The Cruel Years

The Cruel Years

AMERICAN VOICES AT THE DAWN
OF THE TWENTIETH CENTURY

Edited by

WILLIAM LOREN KATZ

and

LAURIE R. LEHMAN

Beacon Press
Boston

Beacon Press
25 Beacon Street
Boston, Massachusetts 02108-2892
www.beacon.org

Beacon Press books
are published under the auspices of
the Unitarian Universalist Association of Congregations.

07 06 05 04 03   8 7 6 5 4 3 2 1

This book is printed on acid-free paper that meets the
uncoated paper ANSI/NISO specifications for permanence
as revised in 1992.

Excerpts reprinted from *The Rebel Girl: An Autobiography* by
Elizabeth Gurley Flynn, with permission from International Publishers, New York, NY.

Excerpts reprinted from *Memoirs* by Bernardo Vega, with permission
from Monthly Review Press, New York, NY.

Photographs are from the collection of William Loren Katz.

Library of Congress Cataloging-in-Publication Data

The cruel years : American voices at the dawn of the twentieth century /
    edited by William Loren Katz and Laurie R. Lehman
      p. cm.
    Originally published: New York : Apex Press . . . c2001
    Includes bibliographical references.
    ISBN 0-8070-5453-4
      1. United States—Social conditions—1865–1918. 2. Poor—
    United States—History—Sources. 3. Poor—United States—
    Biography. I. Katz, William Loren. II. Lehman, Laurie R.

HN57.C783 2003
306'.0973—dc21   2002038649

To those twenty-two men and women whose extraordinary lives appear in these pages; and to Tamara Dembo, Steve Nelson and Esther and James Jackson: they tried to build a better United States.

Contents

Preface by Howard Zinn

William Loren Katz has pioneered in the presentation of little-known history—especially of African Americans and Native Americans—to the American public. In this book he uses his considerable experience as a historical detective to let us hear the words, not of generals, industrialists, and political leaders, but of working people, whose voices are ignored in traditional histories: men, women, immigrants, the native-born, factory workers, farmers, miners, meatpackers, Native Americans, and African Americans. These ordinary men and women tell their personal stories of living in an America which too often did not pay attention to them.

Preface

The voices we hear in these pages are those of the turn of the nineteenth century, a time of extraordinary trouble and turmoil. But trouble and turmoil were not new to this country. We can go back to the late 1700s and early 1800s and find a different set of situations, but also fundamental truths about America common to both periods.

In that earlier time, manufacturing was still in its infancy, there was not yet a great rush of people from farms to cities, and there were no Titans of industry and finance like Morgan, Rockefeller, or Carnegie. The western frontier had not yet closed in on the Indians, the country was not yet flooded with millions of immigrants from Europe. There were no national farmers organizations, no great labor struggles. There was no powerful socialist movement, no migration of African Americans from the South into Northern cities, no drive to expand American influence into the Caribbean, or to take colonies in the Pacific Ocean.

But there were premonitions of all these developments in the early decades of the nation that had just won its independence from England. White workers, slaves, Indians—who are mostly invisible to us today, their words unheard—struggled to survive in a country they did not control.

The nation had come into existence with the stirring language of the Declaration of Independence, a manifesto of democracy. It promised an equal right to "life, liberty, and the pursuit of happiness." However, those noble words concealed harsh realities about the American colonies that rebelled against England.

The Declaration of Independence, pretending to national unity against British rule, gave little indication that American society had long been riven by internal conflicts, between rich and poor, landlords and tenants, the propertied and the propertyless. Those conflicts surfaced during the Revolutionary War, when soldiers in the Pennsylvania and New Jersey lines mutinied, angered by the miserable conditions under which they fought, while serving under officers who were well fed, well uniformed, well paid, and while civilian merchants profiteered from the war.

After the war, class resentment erupted again, especially in Western Massachusetts, where farmers, many of them veterans of the Revolutionary War, rebelled in 1786 against high taxes ("rates"), foreclosures, and loss of their land and livestock. The words of one of the rebels, Plough Jogger, have been kept alive:

> I have been greatly abused, have been obliged to do more than my part in the war; been loaded with class rates, town rates, province rates, Continental rates and all rates . . . been pulled and hauled by sheriffs, constables and collectors, and had my cattle sold for less than they were worth. . . . The great men are going to get all we have and I think it is time for us to rise and put a stop to it, and have no more courts, nor sheriffs, nor collectors nor lawyers. . . .

That uprising was suppressed by force, but the conflict between rich and poor was to continue in the early decades of the new Republic.

Mill girls in the 1830s in Lowell, Massachusetts, and other cities, who worked twelve to sixteen hours a day, conducted strikes to try to better their lives.

The voices of those early labor organizers were heard only with difficulty. But they refused to be silenced. The young women of the New England mills wrote articles and poems for their own publications, *The Factory Girl* and *The Voice of Industry,* which can still be located today in some libraries.

The enslavement of Africans was the most damning contradiction of the claim of the new American nation to democracy. Slavery in the Northern states took a long time to disappear in the years following the Revolution. Racial segregation in the North continued, up to and beyond the Civil War, and even after the passage of the Thirteenth, Fourteenth, and Fifteenth Amendments.

For Indians, the new nation was a disaster. When the British were defeated, the white man moved into Indian territory, and used force to drive the Indians out. The entire continent was now to be opened to invasion.

The voices of Indians remain suppressed for the most part, but the words of the Cherokees, protesting their removal, have been kept alive. They addressed the American nation as follows:

> We are aware that some persons suppose it will be for our advantage to remove beyond the Mississippi. We think otherwise. Our people universally think otherwise. . . . We wish to remain on the land of our fathers. . . . We intreat those to whom the foregoing paragraphs are addressed, to remember the great law of love. "Do to others as ye would that others should do to you."

However, those who dominated the U.S. political system were not interested in listening to the oppressed. By the turn of the twentieth century industrial Robber Barons guided a massive manfacturing march that imposed harsh new forms of economic subjugation. Texts have celebrated this economic elite as brash, diligent, hard-working public benefactors, but have ignored how their ruthless ways crushed labor and undermined democratic government.

People who sweated in mines, mills, or fields to provide vital services during this early industrial age have not been heard. But as this collection shows, with diligent searching, the voices of ordinary people of that extraordinarily troublesome time can still be found, here and there. They tell us of their lives, their fears, and their hopes. Their history is a history to make us think about people who may now be invisible to us, but whose fate is bound up with ours.

That is why we need to listen to the voices William Loren Katz and his collaborator, Laurie R. Lehman, have assembled in this remarkable collection. Hearing the words of these people is a requirement for a truly democratic society.

THE CRUEL YEARS

Introduction by William Loren Katz

We have been left with colorful images of the United States that slipped from the nineteenth into the twentieth century—laughing riders racing through the snow on a horse-drawn buggy; an ornate parlor with flickering gaslights where men in dark suits smoke cigars and discuss business; family picnics on the sunny banks of a blue lake; ladies in tightly laced dresses waltzing at a costume ball. Life was like that—for some.

"In Search of Work"

But for most American families it was a time of wrenching change, economic want, and agonizing stress. By the end of

1893, the nation had entered its worst depression until that time: 3 million wage-earners in a workforce of 15 million lost their jobs, a third of the railroads with 22,500 miles of track fell into receivership, and 32 iron and steel companies and 642 banks closed. In sparsely settled Colorado 30,000 were jobless. Chicago's 200,000 unemployed had to sleep on stairways, floors, or in police stations.

In the home of the brave, confused, discouraged, and frightened families poked in garbage dumps for food. In New York's Union Square fiery young Emma Goldman told a crowd that those with children had a right to seize food from stores. She was arrested for advocating "revolution, violence and bloodshed," and a judge, "on behalf of 'free American institutions,'" sentenced her to a year in Blackwell's Island prison.

By 1894, economic misery had triggered riots and sent 750,000 workers onto picket lines. When the Pullman Company of Illinois declared a large dividend for its stockholders and then cut employees' wages 25 percent, the new American Railway Union and its president, Eugene Debs, began a boycott of Pullman cars that radiated out of Chicago's twenty-four lines and halted rail service nationwide.

U.S. attorney general Richard Olney, whose last job had been as a banker and director of two large railroads, ordered that Pullman Palace cars be attached to mail trains. When strikers halted the mail trains, Olney had his excuse. He sought federal injunctions that led to the imprisonment of Debs and other strike leaders. President Grover Cleveland sent in U.S. troops to quell "a revolution," and the strike was crushed by federal power. A poem in the publication of

Introduction

the American Federation of Labor captured labor's gloomy mood:

Starving in a land of plenty
Hunger-lines on haggard faces
Thousands tramping on and on—
In search of work in far off places.

Civil War veterans mobilized poor people on both coasts to march on Washington and demand work projects or relief during the hard times. "Political liberty is a mockery where economic slavery exists," read their petition to the U.S. Senate.

Into this boiling cauldron walked the world's greatest migration. By the mid-1890s a million men, women, and children a year, largely society's uprooted from eastern and southern Europe, arrived in packed ships and settled in crowded urban slums. Millions of Americans in rural areas were also drawn to cities for work where they jostled the newcomers for jobs and breathing space.

Who were the American people at this time? The 1900 U.S. Census counted 76 million people. There were 9 million African Americans, perhaps as many Hispanic Americans, 237,000 Native Americans, 80,000 Chinese Americans, and 23,000 Japanese Americans. About 26 million white people had been born abroad or to foreign-born parents.

Life for most individuals in the United States was brutish and short. Only 10 percent of adults could read. The average life span was forty-seven, and for people of color it was thirty-four years. Four out of five families were poor, and in his 1904 study, *Poverty,* Robert Hunter revealed that 10 million Americans were "underfed, underclothed, and poorly housed."

Saving was hard. In 1894, a committee that represented millions of underpaid, part-time, and unemployed laboring men from Indiana to California reported that the average wealth of its members "would not purchase a decent coffin." More than 50,000 men wandered country roads begging, seeking work, and committing crimes of poverty. Homeless people were a fixed part of large cities.

Disorder, change, and exploitation marked most lives. For the first time there were fewer farm workers than non–farm workers. Cities were rapidly overtaking rural regions in population and power. The public was bitterly divided over distinctions of identity, class, and race. Men and women appeared to inhabit adjacent, different, and conflicting worlds.

Rapid industrialization sharpened class divisions and created more class violence than ever before. From 1881 to 1900, 6 million workers took part in 2,378 strikes, many of which ended after employers summoned club-wielding police, armed sheriffs, or state militia units. In 1897, the United Mine Workers in Pennsylvania, with 10,000 members, called a strike and 150,000 miners answered the call. Matters were settled when a sheriff and his 102 deputies opened fire without warning on 500 marching strikers, killing 21 and wounding 40 in what was to be called "the Lattimer Massacre."

Laborers began to devise new strategies. In 1900, wives and sisters of Hungarian American strikers in the anthracite coal fields taunted the men hired to replace their husbands and brothers. One strikebreaker angrily described the women: "They ate garlic every morning and spat in our faces when we came out from work in the evening. . . . The gang of women followed us, hooting and hissing, for nearly a mile."

"Where Is Our Share?"

Urban growth was part of a vast social upheaval that left few lives unchanged. A nation of small farms, skilled artisans, and hand-produced goods was being rudely elbowed aside by modern industrialism. Mining and mill jobs increased, and women and men left home to work. No longer did fathers work at home or families have much time to spend together.

Industrial jobs with regular paychecks lured farming folk to glittering cities. They abandoned a rural life of dull, unrelenting drudgery lacking challenge, excitement, and advancement. They were drawn to the bright lights and an urban pace that seemed to dance to the new ragtime beat.

Urban life reshaped the social and political landscape of the United States. By 1900, New York City alone had a population greater by far than the five largest American cities of 1860 combined. But New York's laboring families crowded into dilapidated tenements close to the smell and noise of their work. One small Manhattan tenement had 91 children and 101 adults. Gotham Court apartments at 36 Cherry Street offered large families two-room flats—one room, nine by fourteen, the other, nine by six feet—without plumbing, heat, or sunlight. This was considered a spacious home for a family of five and a suitable one for eight people. Each night as Jacob Riis, author of *How the Other Half Lives*, walked his reporter's beat, he marveled at the capacity of human beings to survive: "The wonder is that they are not all corrupted, and speedily, by their surroundings."

The unemployed, dispossessed, and disheartened as well as the adventurous had abandoned fresh country air. In Pittsburgh they lived next to 14,000 chimneys that killed, said a Hungarian visitor, "everything that grows—trees, grass and flowers." On a visit to Chicago, writer Rudyard Kipling said, "Its air is dirty . . . I never desire to see it again."

In New York City, factories, steam engines, and refineries produced nauseous clouds of sulfur, ammonia gases, and acid fumes that circled the island and never seemed to leave. Each of the city's 150,000 horses daily produced twenty pounds of manure. Manure became floating dust that spread coughs, sickness, and depression. In August 1896 a heat wave killed three thousand people and two thousand horses.

Some dangers moved swiftly. Railroad owners won the right to lay tracks through city streets and in one year the steam locomotives that thundered through Chicago streets took 330 lives. In Manhattan a lone New York Central train turned busy, teeming streets such as Canal, Fourteenth, and Forty-second into what residents called "Death Avenue." By 1908 Central's roaring engine established a world record with 325 deaths (including those of more than 150 children), and left hundreds maimed.

For twenty-five years citizens protested the carnage of "Death Avenue." More than a hundred bills were introduced to the state legislature to condemn the company or force it to elevate its trains. A railroad lobby derailed each effort. In 1909 journalist Charles Edward Russell said of Death

Avenue's victims, "If they had been rich they could have met bribery with bribery, lobby with lobby, influence with influence. . . . Being but poor they must submit to the monstrous perversion of justice and law-making that always and inevitably attends the gathering of huge wealth by illegitimate means."

By 1910, immigrants formed a seventh of the United States population, and made up 20 million of 45 million city dwellers. Their presence shaped urban life, but often in unpredictable ways. Ethnic rivalry, crowding, and job insecurity turned cities into tinderboxes needing only a spark. Newspapers and politicians routinely blamed urban decay and corruption on these "greenhorns" who inhabited the slums, crowded the jails, and, in return for small favors, voted for the candidates of political bosses. Investigative journalist Lincoln Steffens, however, studied corruption in city after city and found that "the machine controls the whole process of voting, and practices fraud at every stage." Neither foreigners nor the poor, he concluded, but business interests "by bribery, corruption or somehow" controlled urban political machines and governments. In Philadelphia, "the most American of our cities," Steffens found voting lists padded with the names of "dead dogs, children, and non-existent persons."

Each large city claimed at least one crowded, unsanitary slum. Cleveland had the Flats, St. Louis Clabber Ally, New York the Lower East Side, Boston the North End, and Chicago the stockyard district. Slow and inefficient garbage pickup left residents surrounded by their waste. Apartment plumbing leaked and cellars sent sewer gasses upward. Stairs were about to collapse and refuse was piled in hallways. During summer windowless rooms sent residents nightly onto fire escapes or into streets panting for fresh air. During real emergencies, New York's fire commissioner found, most fire escapes, commercial and residential, were "absolutely useless."

For landlords, including the urban financial and political elite, and leading churches, slum rentals were a financial success. Tenement rents, a third higher per square foot than apartments for the affluent, produced profits of fifty percent or more. Landlords justified overcrowding by claiming, in the words of one, "there is no use giving them anything decent, for they weren't used to decent surroundings and would not appreciate them if they had them." In 1884, 43,000 slum families unable to pay the rent were evicted, and the number continued to rise.

Once they left their homes, the poor concentrated on surviving during the working day. Laborers, including 2 million children and 5 million women, faced low pay and repetitious tasks, sudden wage cuts, and unemployment. As they entered factories each morning they saw faces pressed against the gates, people eager to take their jobs, and at less pay.

For as little as four or five cents an hour, men and women labored twelve hours a day, six days a week. Steel plants offered twelve-hour shifts seven days a week. In poorly lit, unventilated, and unsafe mines and mills, children and adults tried to meet the demands of untiring machines, irritable foremen, and absentee owners focused on profits. Miners faced lethal cave-ins, and in the month of December 1906 three different U.S. disasters took 663 miners' lives and injured hundreds of others. Yet daughter followed mother and son followed father into mine or mill, and often into an early grave. Some men and women were old at thirty, others died of overwork, and injuries cast many into early retirement.

In 1910, women and girls made up a fifth of those employed in manufacturing. Most failed to earn the five hundred dollars a year that was the official federal poverty level. For the same work factories paid men $1.75 a day and women $1.25. And women laborers, many described as "pale, narrow-chested" or having "drawn white faces, and stooping gait," had to return each day to cook, clean, and care for family, home, and children. Chicago mill inspector Florence Kelly reported: "It is no rare thing for girls to faint at their work . . . suffering exhaustion after working sixteen, eighteen and even twenty hours in heat and dampness in ill-ventilated laundries." To support their families thousands of employed women were also driven to prostitution.

Mothers who worked outside the home had to leave their children alone, or in the care of relatives or strangers. Tens of thousands of urban women labored at home over sewing machines in return for a few pennies for completed garments. Their little children assisted them as best they could, picking up, gathering, and bringing.

Child poverty defined urban life. In 1908, in Chicago, a Board of Education official found five thousand children "habitually hungry," ten thousand without "sufficiently nourishing food," and thousands more under six "underfed." He wrote: "Many of the children lack shoes and clothing. Many have no beds to sleep in. They huddle together on hard floors . . . live in damp, unclean or overcrowded homes, that lack proper ventilation and sanitation."

At work children faced the same hazards as adults. In 1903, New York City superintendent of education William Maxwell reported "children five and six years old . . . at the hardest and most trying kind of labor." In a textile factory, a government investigator found one child "fifty inches high and weighing perhaps forty-eight pounds, who works from six at night until six in the morning, and is so tiny that she has to climb up on the spinning frame to reach the top row of spindles." As a child in New York, Pauline Newman worked for years in a garment factory that had only one visit by an inspector: "we youngsters were hidden in wooden cases covered with shirt waists and told not to move."

In Chicago's canning factories, an inspector reported, "not a day passes but some child is made a helpless cripple." Most accidents took place after 3 p.m., he found, when the young "can no longer direct their tired fingers and aching arms with any degree of accuracy" and become "a prey of the great cutting knives, or the jaws of the tin-stamping machines." Managers of the Chicago stockyards offered a benefit policy for men who suffered serious injuries while engaged in dangerous work: their sons, some fourteen and under, were allowed to take their jobs until they could return.

The factory accident rate for children was double the adult rate. In 1903, "Mother" Mary Jones reported from Pennsylvania: "Every day little children come into Union Headquarters, some with hands cut off, some with the thumb missing, some with their fingers off at the knuckle.

Introduction

They were stooped little things, round shouldered and skinny."

Employers were pleased to hire children for mines and mill work, since they were paid lower wages than adults—often fifty cents a week well into the new century—and often for the same work. Moralists and ministers stepped forward to claim mill jobs, kept little ones out of trouble, and taught them useful, adult habits. Asa G. Candlers, founder of Coca-Cola, said: "The most beautiful sight that we see is the child at labor; as early as he may be at labor the more beautiful, and the most useful does his life get to be."

Working children had a different view. In 1903, children in a Philadelphia textile plant unfurled these protest banners: "We Want to Go to School!" "More Schools Less Hospitals!" "Prosperity! Where Is Our Share?" Untold numbers of children had no known addresses and had to fend for themselves. In 1880, an estimated 100,000 New York City children were homeless, and their number grew each decade. Some were hired as messengers, servants, and thieves; others sold matches, newspapers, and their services.

Many took any job that paid. As they scrounged for food and searched for shelter, many were brutalized by adults or other children whose predatory instincts had been honed in the battle for survival.

Unsafe working conditions took a fearful toll on the U.S. workforce. More than a million men and women died or were injured each year at work, a higher number than in any other country in the world that kept records. In 1892, President Benjamin Harrison observed, "American workmen are subjected to peril of life and limb as great as a soldier in time of war."

In 1900, railroad laborers endured 2,675 deaths and 41,142 injuries. Managers denied the need for and did not install safety devices, and refused compensation to victims. In 1911, a fire swept through the Triangle Shirt Waist Company in New York City. Exits had been sealed shut to keep out union organizers, and in eighteen minutes 146 young Italian and Jewish immigrant women died, plunging out of windows or overcome by smoke pressed against doors that did not open. Rose Schneiderman, who the year before had organized the workers and had seen them beaten and jailed for union activities, spoke at their memorial: "Every week I must learn of the untimely death of one of my sister workers. Every year thousands of us are maimed."

In the battle over wages, hours, and working conditions, industry stacked all the weapons. The term "captains of industry" had a pure meaning. Corporation executives hired armies of detectives to fight their employees and recruited spies to infiltrate and disrupt their unions. "I can hire one half the working class to kill the other half," boasted financier Jay Gould, a manipulator of legislators and judges. A media sympathetic to the wealthy portrayed workmen's compensation, unemployment insurance, and paid vacations as pipe dreams proposed by soft-hearted reformers or alien revolutionaries.

By 1900, less than 2 percent of U.S. workers were enrolled in trade unions, and most of these were skilled white men recruited by the American Federation of Labor. Its president, Samuel Gompers, a recent immigrant, advocated "racial purity," did not recruit people of color, the unskilled, and women, and boasted of his role in persuading the U.S. Congress to ban Chinese immigration.

Introduction

At a time when businessmen wielded enormous power, U.S. workers were bitterly divided. During the 1890s white workers staged fifty strikes to keep African Americans from working alongside them. Blocked from union membership and decent jobs, a person of color often found his or her only chance for decent work was to serve as a strikebreaker.

Since the 1830s trade unions had been stripped of their power by a judicial system that considered strikes and unions to be conspiracies "to injure trade." This conspiracy definition allowed companies to summon police, state militia, and ultimately call for federal injunctions and U.S. troops.

Politicians, clergymen, and newspaper editors roundly condemned strikes and occasionally urged cold-blooded violence against union activities. Respected Brooklyn minister Henry Ward Beecher spoke candidly: "If the club of the policeman, knocking out the brains of the rioter, will answer, then well and good; but if it does not promptly meet the exigency, then bullets and bayonets, canister and grape . . . constitute the one remedy. . . . Napoleon was right when he said the way to deal with a mob is to exterminate it."

When New York horsecar drivers working sixteen hours a day for twelve dollars a week sought a reduction to twelve hours, state legislator Theodore Roosevelt called their demand "communistic."

"You Are Tracked with Bloodhounds"

If working and living conditions were barely tolerable for the majority of white men, women, and children, they often proved unbearable for people of color. The 1890s opened at Wounded Knee, South Dakota, with the massacre of 350 Lakota men, women, and children surrounded by the U.S. Seventh Cavalry. "We tried to run," said one of the fifty survivors, "but they shot us like we were buffalo." For their part in the slaughter, 18 U.S. Cavalrymen were awarded the Congressional Medal of Honor.

Great Native American nations were herded onto government-run reservations, there to watch helplessly as missionaries undermined their culture, religion, and families. T. J. Morgan, commissioner of Indian Affairs, stated: "We ask them to recognize that we are the better race; that our God is the true God; that our civilization is the better; that our manners and customs are superior."

In 1887, Congress passed an Allotment Act that divided millions of acres of reservation land into individual holdings. The aim was to compel people unfamiliar with capitalism to accept individual ownership. Instead 90 million acres of Indian land fell into the hands of white speculators. "The love of possession," Sitting Bull said of whites, "is a disease with them."

As the old century turned into the new, the White House served as a fountainhead of racial animosity. President Cleveland announced that African Americans were too ignorant to vote, and he favored racially segregated schools north and south. Teddy Roosevelt called African Americans "a perfectly stupid race" and "altogether inferior to whites." Addressing African American college graduates in North Carolina in 1909, William Howard Taft said, "Your race is adapted to be a race of farmers, first, last, and for all time." No president tried to enforce the Fourteenth

Amendment to the Constitution that protected African American voting rights.

By the early twentieth century 90 percent of African Americans lived in the South as landless, disenfranchised peasants. The forces of white supremacy had overthrown a brief postwar effort to bring republican government and equality to the region. South Carolina's "Pitchfork" Ben Tillman boasted to his fellow U.S. senators of how his state used brutality and fraud to deny African Americans their constitutional rights: "We have done our level best; we have scratched our heads to find out how we could eliminate the last one of them. We stuffed ballot boxes. We shot them. We are not ashamed of it."

As the governmental arm of the former slave masters, the Democratic party controlled the eleven southern states. Though slavery had ended it was quickly replaced by two new tyrannies: the sharecropping system and convict lease system. When sharecroppers dared to flee their work, they were hunted down by sheriffs' posses and returned to their employers much as slave runaways had been.

The convict lease system, designed to keep taxes low for white citizens, turned a vast prison system into a free labor supply. Courts imposed five-year jail sentences on African Americans for petty or nonexistent crimes, then prisoners were rented out. "The court and the man you work for are always partners," recounted one victim. "One makes the fine and the other works you and holds you, and if you leave you are tracked with bloodhounds and brought back." For twenty cents a day the Tennessee Coal, Iron and Railroad Company leased each of the state's thirteen hundred convicts. Untold numbers of prisoners were worked to death or died from other forms of cruelty instituted by state officials and mine supervisors.

Beginning in 1890, southern states altered their constitutions to disenfranchise African Americans and to impose racial segregation in jobs, public facilities, and transportation. In 1896 in the *Plessy v. Ferguson* case the U.S. Supreme Court, with one dissenting jurist, ruled this U.S. version of apartheid did not violate the Constitution. Segregation remained the law of the land until 1954.

Southern politicians tolerated and many encouraged racial violence. Mobs, often led by law enforcement officers and goaded on by clergymen, senators, and governors, lynched African Americans with impunity. "If it is necessary, every Negro in the state will be lynched. It will be done to maintain white supremacy," declared Governor James Vardaman of Mississippi. From 1889 to 1901 more than two thousand African American men—and sometimes women and children—died at the hands of mobs. In many instances "lynching bees"—carnivals of torture and death to which white women and children were invited and refreshments were served—defined southern racial relations. President Roosevelt, who did little even in word to discourage lynchings, sternly warned African American audiences that the criminals and rapists among them did more harm "than any white man can possibly do them."

In 1898, a white supremacy political campaign in Wilmington, North Carolina, was followed by a riot that drove African American officeholders and many families from the city. Wilmington introduced a quarter century of coordinated, daylight, white invasions of African American neighborhoods, similar to Russian and Polish "pogroms" that drove millions of Jews into exile. In 1906 Atlanta, a symbol of "New South" tolerance, was paralyzed for four days as a surging white mob killed nine people and injured hundreds of others. By 1908, murderous riots had spread northward to Springfield, Illinois, and lynchings took place a few blocks from where Abraham Lincoln once lived.

Poll taxes, literacy tests, and property qualifications designed to terminate the constitutional rights of African Americans were also used to eliminate the political power of poor whites. White laborers were denied the vote, a chance to earn a decent wage, join a union, or organize for their own goals.

Racism was a national problem. African Americans were portrayed degradingly in magazines, newspapers, popular songs, nursery rhymes, and jokes. No African American was elected to Congress from the South after 1898, and none from the North until 1928. In 1900, a St. Louis Bible society published a book, *Is the Negro a Beast?*, that sought to prove that people of African descent lacked a soul. The best advice educator Booker T. Washington, the leading African American spokesman of the day, could offer his people was, "When your head is in the lion's mouth, use your hand to pet him."

In Texas and the Southwest, Mexican Americans also faced treatment as citizens without rights or dignity. Forced to accept U.S. rule after the Mexican War they found they had no legal standing, and were victims of a popular, armed militia known as "Texas Rangers." They labored for low wages, without benefits, and lived under a state-sponsored terror designed by their employers.

Fear of recent immigrants who were arriving in large numbers from southern and eastern Europe also stoked a rise in anti-Catholicism and anti-Semitism. In 1891, a mob murdered eleven Italian prisoners being held for trial in the New Orleans Parish Prison. In Troy, New York, a week later another mob attacked a meeting called by Italian Americans to protest the massacre.

The 1890s gave birth to a bigoted American Protective Association (APA), which claimed millions of members, including a hundred congressmen. The APA demanded passage of federal laws to restrict immigration and to limit voting rights to men who spoke English and lived in the United States for at least seven years. APA meetings sparked riots in Iowa, Missouri, Georgia, and New York. However, when the organization endorsed William McKinley for president, and its members learned that the new president had Catholic friends, the APA dissolved in angry disputes.

The decade ended as it had begun, in a crescendo of racial violence. In 1900, 105 African Americans were lynched by mobs. That year whites rampaged through New Orleans for three days hunting down and killing African Americans. In midtown Manhattan that year police initiated two days of assaults on African Americans. The official police cover-up convinced many African Americans to move to a safe, uptown community named Harlem. Two years later in New York, Irish Americans attacked Jewish Americans who had entered their neighborhood to attend a rabbi's funeral. The official report noted that police led the assault and conducted "the most brutal clubbing."

Though New York City had been a multicultural city from the arrival of Henry Hudson's *Half Moon,* Police

Commissioner Theodore Bingham took a dim view of some of those he was sworn to protect. "Jews went into crime because they were unfit for hard labor," he said, and Italians were a "riffraff of desperate scoundrels, ex-convicts, and jailbirds."

"Corruption at the Very Source of Power"

By 1890, the U.S. became the world's leading producer of iron and steel, and nine years later the largest producer of coal. Between 1898 and 1903 small firms increasingly were swallowed by large ones and a record 276 new corporations were charted. One, U.S. Steel, owned by J. P. Morgan, became the first billion-dollar company when it fused eleven mining and shipping companies from coast to coast.

Monopolies and trusts dominated economic life. In 1904, 318 trusts controlled $7 billion in capital and 40 percent of U.S. industry. Through their seats on dozens of corporation boards of directors a few men ruled the country's economy. Morgan sat on forty-eight business boards and John D. Rockefeller on thirty-seven.

At the pinnacle of the U.S. economic and political pyramid stood a wealthy elite. Less than two generations after the Civil War, the country's largest fortunes had soared tenfold and twenty-fold. By 1901 at least thirty men owned a billion and a half dollars or more, and thousands of others had become millionaires. One percent of the population owned as much as the other 99 percent. Chicago merchant Marshall Field made six hundred dollars an hour and paid clerks at his retail stores three to five dollars a week after three years of satisfactory service.

When business tycoons called the tune influential clergymen, governors, and editors danced, and the White House listened attentively. The song's refrain was that poverty was a sin and wealth a sign of virtue and heavenly favor. In 1907, John D. Rockefeller announced, "I am the trustee of the property of others, through the providence of God committed to my care."

Others agreed. "Godliness is in league with riches," said William Lawrence, Episcopal bishop of Massachusetts. "To make money honestly is to preach the Gospel," announced Reverend Russell H. Conwell in his famous lecture "Acres of Diamonds." He became rich publicly delivering his paean to wealth more than six thousand times.

The affluent wrapped themselves in a patriotic garb and offered few excuses for their excesses. Steel magnate Chauncey Depew could rise late each day, but his mill laborers began work at six in the morning, worked twelve-hour shifts seven days a week in 115 or more degrees of heat for a salary of $1.25 a day. Depew announced: "The laboring man in this bounteous and hospitable country has no grounds for complaint."

The powerful often explained their dubious morality and questionable legality by claiming the blessings of heaven. When Benjamin Harrison, a Presbyterian deacon, was elected to the White House, he proclaimed, "Providence has given us the victory." Matthew Quay, his campaign manager, knew better. "Providence didn't have a damn thing to do with it," Quay said, since he knew many men who "were compelled to approach the gates of penitentiary to make him President."

Introduction

Newspapers and magazines glorified business successes. In 1885, the *Chicago Tribune* applauded people "seized with the craze for money making" and welcomed "large profits, and everything apparently inviting [people] to be rich." That year the Southern Methodist Publishing House issued William Speer's *The Law of Success,* which emphasized "the commercial value of the Ten Commandments." Speer claimed "the educator of the future will teach his pupils what will pay best . . . the art of turning one's brains into money." In 1900, the *New York Times* welcomed the new century with these words: "Millionaires will be commonplace and the country will be better for them, better for their wealth, better for the good they will do in giving employment to labor in the industries which produce their fortunes."

Corporations pursued profits without regard to the human cost. There were only five national parks in 1900 and half of the country's forests fell before the axes of powerful lumber barons. In the Gulf states where lumber output rose fivefold a U.S. forestry expert referred to this as "probably the most rapid and reckless destruction of forests known to history." Senator Robert La Follette told Congress how Wisconsin's lumber industry operated: "They . . . organized their lumber trust; they exploited the people of Wisconsin. . . . They devastated the northern half of the State. . . . These great lumber corporations, enriched by the despoliation of our natural resources in Wisconsin, became the dictators of the public policy of the State."

Federal and state officials, in the name of progress, offered cheap or free land to rail companies. The federal government gave millions of acres to railroad trusts and speculators. Texas offered twelve rail corporations 32 million acres, an area the size of Indiana.

Businessmen spoke with refreshing candor about the mission and values of their class. Andrew Carnegie, who made $23 million in 1900, said: "We accept and welcome, as conditions to which we must accommodate ourselves great inequality of wealth and environment, the concentration of business, industrial and commercial, in the hands of the few, as being not only beneficial, but essential for the future of the race." Cornelius Vanderbilt repeatedly told journalists: "The public be damned." "Society," intoned Morton H. Smith, president of the Louisville and Nashville Railroad, "was created for the purpose of one man's getting what the other fellow has, if he can, and keep out of the penitentiary."

Legislators, presidents, and judges bowed to the affluent. In 1901, *Bankers' Magazine* announced "the business of the country . . . is gradually subverting the power of the politician and rendering him subservient to its purposes." The U.S. Senate was known as "the Millionaires Club" because it had many millionaire members, was devoted to business interests, and because in selecting their state's two U.S. senators state legislators were open to bribes or swayed by corporate power. When Cornelius Vanderbilt, James Duke, Leland Stanford, Ezra Cornell, and John D. Rockefeller founded colleges that bore their names they were lauded for their devotion to education.

Cornelius Vanderbilt was one of many tycoons who made purchases in the public sector. He boasted that he was able "to buy up any politician," and found reformers "the most purchasable. They don't come so high." During his two terms as President, Teddy Roosevelt called himself a "trust-buster" but his administration prosecuted only one successful anti-trust case, and his chief advisers were three men representing Morgan and three men representing Rockefeller.

Corporation attorneys rewrote the legal system. The Fourteenth Amendment to the Constitution, designed to protect citizenship rights of African Americans after slavery, instead was redesigned to protect corporations. Supreme Court Justice Hugo Black noted that in all the Fourteenth Amendment cases brought before the high court "during the first fifty years after its adoption [in 1868], less than one half of one percent invoked it in the protection of the Negro race, and more than fifty percent asked that its benefits be extended to corporations."

When industry confronted labor in the courts, it held all the cards. "We hire the law by the year," boasted a railroad owner. The Sherman Act of 1890 was passed to curb monopolies but the judiciary permitted corporate attorneys to use its injunctions to crush strikes and jail union leaders. In fifty years 1,800 of its injunctions were issued against strikers and unions, and there was little effort at evenhandedness: between 1901 and 1928, of 118 federal courts injunctions used against strikes, 70 were issued by judges who did not notify the union defendants, or refused them an opportunity to argue their case.

Union leaders protested in vain. "[T]rust magnates have captured the benefits for themselves, either through prostrated courts, bribed legislators, or using the gatling gun whenever organized labor demanded a small portion of their product," complained union leader Isaac Cowen.

When businessmen's profits were at stake laws passed for one purpose were reshaped to serve another. The Interstate Commerce Act, designed to regulate business practices harmful to the public, had a different effect. It did little more than lull the growing clamor for control of trusts. For this reason, Attorney General Olney told a rail tycoon, this law was "of great use to the railroads."

Corporations also could rely on government officials to tell their story. When a choking industrial smog blanketed the city of Chicago, a leading politician said smoke was beneficial to children's lungs. In 1892, a Texas court in a ruling against workers said: "Unquestionably, so long as men must earn a living for their families and themselves by labor, there must be . . . oppression of the working classes." Circuit court judge William Howard Taft was hardly impartial in 1894 when he had to rule on the Pullman strike.

Privately he wrote to his wife that it was a "most outrageous strike," wanted it to "fail miserably," wished for "much bloodletting," rejoiced when troops shot thirty strikers, and hoped they would "kill" more.

The Democrat or Republican in the White House could be counted on to support the rich and powerful rather than the public. In 1887, President Grover Cleveland, with a large gold surplus on hand, vetoed a bill to give seed grain to Texas farmers stricken by a drought. Such aid, he stated, "encourages the expectation of paternal care on the part of government and weakens the sturdiness of our national character." Instead the President used the surplus to ensure that rich bondholders received $45 million more than the value of their bonds. Evidently he was not worried about the impact on their character.

In this age of jarring industrial and financial expansion and sudden individual wealth, the United States created its first "welfare state" to safeguard the wealthy and their trusts. Businessmen returned the favor. On the Saturday before the presidential election in 1896 five thousand New York City bankers and brokers donned silk black hats and marched under 108-foot American flags in a parade for presidential candidate William McKinley. U.S. corporations taxed themselves a staggering $16 million to guarantee his victory.

Wealth continued to dominate U.S. elections. Thirty years later Republican senator William Borah called money "the moving power of American politics" and "a fearful national evil." He saw "corruption at the very source of power."

"A Hateful Oligarchy of Sex"

If working people lived at the mercy of bosses, middle-class and even affluent wives and daughters also had to abide by rules set by a society ruled by men. Many courts accorded women the legal status of children. Kitchen and bedroom were their prison.

Male experts of the day categorized women "as closer to savages and children than adult civilized males." A Harvard professor claimed attending college would "destroy a woman's reproductive organs." In 1901, in *The Independent,* Henry Finch warned: "Women's participation in political life would involve the domestic calamity of a deserted home and the loss of the womanly qualities for which refined men adore women and marry them. . . . Doctors tell us, too, that thousands of children would be harmed or killed before birth by the injurious effect of untimely political excitement on their mothers."

For women of color, white male judgment was even harsher. The *Independent* stated that African American women "were steeped in centuries of ignorance and savagery, and wrapped about with immoral vices."

Winter and summer a proper ladylike attire was fifteen yards of floor-sweeping clothing finished in the back with a large padded bustle. Layers of undergarments included a steel reinforced corset that pressed twenty-one to eighty-eight pounds of metal against flesh and bone. Harmful and dangerous to the wearer's health, it produced a shape men desired, and served as a reminder that even in fashion men were in command.

A host of rigid codes originally shaped by Puritans and compressed into Victorian double standards regulated women's social obligations and manners. It was not acceptable to mention politics, sex, alcoholism, or equal rights. "We were more or less sheltered from everything," recalled one woman, "especially sex." Wives were expected to smile politely through loveless marriages and silently assent to their husbands' desires. In 1915, Sigmund Freud found that the United States had the "most extreme form" of sexual morality, and he termed it "very contemptible."

Except in southern states, women could sue for divorce, but it was a costly and frightening process. Divorced women faced a collapse of finances, a life of moral censure, and possible loss of custody of their children. Despite its man-made marriage codes, divorce rates in the U.S. were higher than those of any other country that kept statistics. Between 1867 and 1906 the divorce rate rose 30 percent every five years while the population increased only 10 percent.

Women had a right to vote only in Utah, Wyoming, Colorado, and Idaho. Elsewhere women's suffrage brought sarcasm and derisive laughter in which women were expected to join. "This government is not a Republic," said one dissenting woman, "but a hateful oligarchy of sex.

Even bike riding created a problem for women of the day: how were they to avoid revealing their ankles during the downstroke? Women bicyclists sought to quiet male anxiety by covering their ankles with thick, high shoes and leather or cloth gaiters.

"Raise Less Corn and More Hell"

Though a wealthy few dominated economic and political life in the United States, their rule did not go unchallenged. In 1887, in his futuristic novel *Looking Backward*, Edward Bellamy warned of the consequences of the "soulless machine, incapable of any motive but insatiable greed." He projected the replacement of capitalism in 1900 by a society that eradicated pauperism, economic suffering, and class distinctions. Protestant ministers launched a "social gospel" movement that rejected capitalism and argued that "Jesus was a socialist."

Henry George, who grew up poor, wrote *Progress and Poverty* to mobilize resistance to "the worship of wealth." Economist Thorstein Veblen wrote *The Theory of Business*

Enterprise to warn that "chronic depression" was "normal" to an unregulated, profit-driven economy. Nebraska congressman William Jennings Bryan pointed out how a rich man's media distorted political language:

> The poor man is called a socialist if he believes that the wealth of the rich should be divided among the poor, but the rich man is called a financier if he devises a plan by which the pittance of the poor can be converted to his use. The poor man who takes property by force is called a thief, but the creditor who can by legislation make a debtor pay a dollar twice as large as he borrowed is lauded as the friend of sound currency. The man who wants the people to destroy the government is an anarchist but the man who wants the government to destroy the people is a patriot.

Many ordinary citizens had begun to see the two-party system as corrupt. In 1915, New York Republican boss William Barnes sued former president Theodore Roosevelt for publicly stating that between 1898 and 1910 (when TR served as governor of New York and president of the United States) a corrupt ring of Democrat and Republican bosses controlled New York state politics. A Syracuse jury ruled in favor of Roosevelt.

The strongest mobilization against corporate manipulation of state and federal power was launched by small western farmers who saw themselves victims of an unfair economic system dominated by the wealthy. The more farmers produced, the lower agricultural prices fell. Corn that sold in 1869 for 75 cents had fallen in 1889 to 28 cents. In 1867 the West's cereal crops of 1.3 million bushels paid producers $1.3 billion, but in 1887 the 2.7 million bushels produced paid only $1.2 billion. At the same time, prices farmers paid for seed, transportation, and machinery rose.

Sudden crop failures, and occasional epidemics of cholera, smallpox, diphtheria, and typhoid also punctuated farmers' hard and lonely toil. In Indiana in 1879 the Reverend Myron Reed found farm wives were "not much better off than slaves." They had to withstand "a weary monotonous round of cooking and washing and mending, and as a result the insane asylum is 1/3 filled with wives of farmers."

Eastern bankers, railroad magnates, and businessmen accelerated the farmers' crisis. From 1889 to 1893 Kansas suffered 11,123 foreclosures. In two years twenty towns closed and banks seized 90 percent of the land in fifteen Kansas counties. One woman pleaded with Governor Lorenzo D. Lewelling, "We are starving to death. . . . I haven't had nothing to eat today and it is three o'clock."

In the South, where nine out of ten farmers lived on credit, conditions were even worse. In 1873 cotton that sold for 15 cents a pound had by 1897 fallen to 5.8 cents. In the Texas Panhandle in 1886 a note on an abandoned cabin read: "250 miles to the nearest post office; 100 miles to wood; 20 miles to water; 6 inches to hell. God bless our home! Gone to live with the wife's folks."

In 1892 poor western and southern farmers united in a People's or Populist Party that proclaimed democracy in peril:

> We meet in the midst of a nation brought to the verge of moral, political and material ruin. Corruption dominates the ballot box, the legislatures, the Congress, and touches even the ermine of the bench. The people are demoralized.

. . . The newspapers are subsidized or muzzled; public opinion silenced; business prostrate, our homes covered with mortgages, labor impoverished, and the land concentrating in the hands of capitalists. . . . From the same prolific womb of governmental injustice we breed two classes—paupers and millionaires.

The party's leading voice, Mary Ellen Lease, of Kansas, told farmers "to raise less corn and more hell" and took aim at a new enemy: "It is no longer a government of the people, by the people, and for the people, but a government of Wall Street, by Wall Street and for Wall Street."

The Populists scored political upsets in the West, and in the South they initially challenged the Democrat's one-party rule when they invited and protected African American voters. After the party won some offices in Georgia and North Carolina, this infuriated the entrenched forces of white supremacy who unleashed a wave of intimidation, lynchings, and riots that ended Black voting rights.

African Americans reached for new leaders and novel forms of resistance. By the 1880s thousands of African American families had fled southern violence to build communities in Kansas, and between 1890 and 1910 Oklahoma boasted thirty all-Black towns. In a dozen southern cities men and women staged "sit-ins" to desegregate horse-drawn streetcars.

In 1892, as lynching rose to three a week, young crusading African American journalist Ida B. Wells used her Memphis Free Speech to launch a crusade against this massive crime. After a mob wrecked her press, she fled Memphis, and for the next four decades carried her anti-lynching campaign into northern states and Europe. In 1900, George Henry White of North Carolina, a former slave and the nineteenth century's last African American congressman, introduced the first federal anti-lynching bill, but it was not reported out of the House Judiciary Committee.

In 1905, W. E. B. Du Bois inaugurated the "Niagara movement" for African American liberation, saying: "We will not be satisfied to take one jot or tittle less than our full manhood rights." In 1909, Du Bois joined white and Black reformers who organized the NAACP to fight discrimination and lynchings.

Jail time and oppression made radicals out of white dissenters. Emma Goldman left prison to become an activist-philosopher of anarchism, a defender of homosexual rights, to be arrested in 1916 for circulating birth control materials, and finally to be deported by the government as an "undesirable alien" in 1919. Once he left prison after the Pullman Strike, Eugene Debs shaped the new Socialist party and five times ran as its presidential candidate. In 1920 and from a federal cell, where he had been jailed for opposing World War I, he garnered almost a million votes.

In 1905 Debs, "Mother" Jones, and other radical labor figures organized the Industrial Workers of the World (IWW). The preamble to the group's charter breathed fire: a war existed between capital and labor, and workers' violence was justified to overthrow corporate rule. As "one big union" the IWW recruited men and women across the flaming lines of race, skill, gender, and ethnicity, and conducted daring strikes that terrified the media, politicians, and the wealthy. When local sheriffs jailed IWW members for speaking in public, others arrived to take their place, cram jails beyond capacity, and win everyone's release.

"A Splendid Little War"

Some of society's privileged saw a day of reckoning in the mounting chaos, unemployment, racial and economic strife, and the rising mobilization of laborers and farmers by Populists and Socialists. In 1889, the Commercial and Financial Chronicle predicted that only by seizing foreign markets could the U.S. economy escape collapse. In 1894, Morgan partner Francis Stetson warned President Cleveland: "We are on the eve of a very dark night unless a return of commercial prosperity relieves popular discontent." Senator William Frye insisted that unless the United States captured Asian markets "we shall have a revolution."

Economic crises at home triggered ventures abroad. In 1893, U.S. businessmen overthrew the government of Hawaii, which had treaties and trade relations with dozens of nations, including the United States. As U.S. attorney general, Richard Olney directed the federal assault that ended the Pullman strike. The next year as secretary of state he proclaimed a U.S. doctrine that ushered in an era of colonial expansion backed by force: "Today the United States is practically sovereign on this continent, and its fiat is law . . ."

Appeals to white supremacy stoked the flames of imperialist conquest. In 1885, influential congregationalist minister Josiah Strong wrote *Our Country* to proclaim a white global destiny at hand. He asked rhetorically if "this race . . . is destined to dispossess many weaker races, assimilate others, and mould the remainder, until, in a very true and important sense, it has Anglo-Saxonized mankind?" His book sold over 100,000 copies.

"I should welcome almost any war, for I think this country needs one," said Teddy Roosevelt, the new assistant secretary of the navy. His list of target countries included Mexico, Chile, Canada, Spain, Germany, and England. Roosevelt was bullish on war as a form of spiritual renewal that would stimulate "the clear instinct for race selfishness." His views on race, manhood, and commerce seemed to blend. "All the great masterful races have been fighting races." He added, "The most ultimately righteous of all wars is a war with savages." People of color were, he noted, "formidable fighters but no match for the white man."

When U.S. statesmen called for war they emphasized a mixture of patriotism and a need for overseas trade. Roosevelt's leading supporter was Senator Albert Beveridge, who spoke of "the mission of our race," called whites "God's chosen people," and referred to colonized people as "children . . . not capable of self-government." Beveridge transformed commercial desperation into patriotic fervor: "American factories are making more than the American people can use; American soil is producing more than they can consume. Fate has written our policy for us; the trade of the world must and shall be ours."

By 1898 U.S. corporations had invested more than $50 million in Cuban plantations and sugar refineries. Though at first many businessmen opposed war, leading newspapers demanded Cuba's liberation from Spanish tyranny. Within the year U.S. battleships steamed into the Caribbean and Pacific to wrest control of Spain's colonial empire. Secretary of War Hay called it "a splendid little war."

Congress's announced aim was to "free" Cuba, but President McKinley had a wider goal: "[W]e must keep all we get; when the war is over we must keep all we want." After ten weeks and only 379 battlefield deaths, the United States laid claim to islands that stretched from Puerto Rico in the Caribbean to the Philippines and Hawaii in the Pacific.

U.S. expansion rested on the bedrock of racial bigotry. The day Congress declared war on Spain, Congressman David A. De Armond of Missouri called African Americans "almost too ignorant to eat, scarcely wise enough to breathe, mere existing human machines." The U.S. Supreme Court that found segregation constitutional five years later ruled in the Downes case that Puerto Ricans and other colonial people could be denied their constitutional rights. The doctrine was devised by Justice Edward White, a Louisiana politician who was still thrilled that he rode as a member of the Ku Klux Klan. Two years later White voted with the court majority in the Lone Wolf case when it ruled Indian treaties could be broken by Congress "if consistent with perfectly good policy toward the Indians."

United States military units were soon arrayed against long-standing liberation movements. To avoid arrest by Spanish officials, Puerto Rican and Cuban refugees such as liberator Jose Marti and Dr. Ramon Betances, "father of Puerto Rican independence," had fled their homelands for

New York City. But long-sought national goals for islanders oppressed by Spain were wrecked with the U.S. arrival.

In the Philippines Emilio Aguinaldo's guerrilla army had battled Spain's colonial armies for two years. After first supporting their liberation efforts, President McKinley dispatched ships and soldiers that prohibited Aguinaldo from marching into Manila, and a U.S. government was installed. Aguinaldo's troops, however, enjoyed widespread support throughout the islands, and it took a well-trained, modern U.S. army of 70,000 three years to defeat a poorly armed foe they called "gooks" and "niggers."

At home opposition mounted to American intervention abroad, particularly among working people and African Americans. Although the Buffalo Soldiers, and other African American units of the U.S. Army served with distinction in the war, African American voices denounced U.S. policy. "I don't think there is a single colored man, out of office or out of the insane asylum, who favors the so-called expansion policy," said Howard University professor Kelley Miller. Bishop Henry M. Turner of the African Methodist Episcopal Church called U.S. claims of humanitarian intervention "too ridiculous to be made a count," and predicted that "all the deviltry of this country would be carried into Cuba the moment the United States got there."

The African American press sided with Aguinaldo. The *Salt Lake City Broad Ax* explained his popularity among his people when it wrote that "maybe the Filipinos have caught wind of the way Indians and Negroes have been Christianized and civilized [by U.S. soldiers]."

The U.S. victory was filled with ironies. Filipino freedom fighters battled an invader who claimed to be bringing Christianity and republicanism. U.S. officers relied on torture and mass murder that did not spare Filipino civilians. Aguinaldo addressed the 6,000 African American U.S. soldiers in the field: "It is without honor that you are spilling your costly blood. Your masters have thrown you into the most iniquitous fight. . . . Your friends the Filipinos, give you good warning. You must consider your situation and your history."

Senator "Pitchfork" Ben Tillman often rose in the Senate to justify white supremacy and lynchings. Now he taunted northern senators for their hypocrisy: "No Republican leader, not even Governor [Theodore] Roosevelt, will now dare wave the bloody shirt and preach a crusade against the South's treatment of the Negro. The North has a bloody shirt of its own. Many thousands of them have been made into shrouds for murdered Filipinos, done to death because they were fighting for liberty."

When U.S. occupation troops were used to smash strikes and jail union leaders from Cuba to the Philippines, U.S. workers saw danger. The journal of the Indianapolis Central Labor Union denounced this "emphatic evidence of military tyranny, if not downright imperialism." Ten weeks after U.S. soldiers first fired on Aguinaldo's supporters, federal troops were sent to Idaho to replace its state's militia, then serving in the Philippines, and fired on striking oil workers. The Carpenter's Union journal declared, "Expansion leads to imperialism which tends to militarism which leads to despotism, and all four lead to oppression and misery for the toiling masses as sure as the sun rises in the east and sets in the west."

This, then, was the United States at the turn of the new century—a land in turmoil, scarred by violence, poverty, and injustice, and about to impose its will on millions of people of color in distant lands.

The chronicles of the United States of America often read less like a complete history of this country than an early version of "the life styles of the rich and famous." The birth of the twentieth century in the United States, for example, usually has been told from the standpoint of those with power, influence, and privilege. The hero often is Teddy Roosevelt, portrayed as a brazen, mercurial figure who led the charge at San Juan Hill, and then from the White House led the charge for conservation and against trusts. But this version omits a great deal, including the contributions, tribulations, and courage of ordinary people whose labor, sacrifice, and grit built the country.

When school texts include common people they are usually commended for their capacity to shoulder hard tasks, serve their country in wartime, and accept their station in life. Their resilient thoughts and resistant spirit are rarely mentioned. That is why, as part of their campaign to reach voters in the 1890s, the Populist party recruited 35,000 lecturers and published dozens of books on economics, politics, and history. "History as taught in our schools," party speakers told all who would listen, "was practically valueless."

Why have the poor or persecuted so infrequently told their own history? Were they too busy? Too inarticulate? Too uninformed? Did they all fade without a trace into the obscurity that surrounded their lives?

Despite formidable handicaps—illiteracy, lack of education, and punishing work schedules—ordinary people did create a written record. It is widely scattered, often fragmented and incomplete, but it exists. People wrote letters to relatives, newspapers, unions, and one another. Some kept diaries and others wrote books. Their words were transcribed, often anonymously and with tantalizing brevity by friends, relatives, and later by journalists, sociologists, and reformers.

Lacking the educational training that gives polish or literary elegance, these Americans nonetheless have something important to say about what they saw, and their messages often resonate with power and emotion. In addition to neglected information, they offer another perspective, sometimes a new world. At times their unadorned words reveal much about unresolved issues, and some individuals are content to merely reflect on their personal struggles to find happiness, leave a mark, and help families survive.

The autobiographical sketches presented here exhibit little tearful despondency. Men and women write or talk of overcoming misfortune, making money, and seeking fulfillment. Some deal with larger political and economic issues and others describe relatives, friends, and romance, or budgeting problems, routines, and leisure time.

Introduction

Contrary to the patriotic biographies offered in school texts these men and women do not pause to "bless America." These narrators are painfully aware of their vulnerability in a society that exploits families for profit. Fearing some kind of retaliation, half refuse to reveal their names.

Immigrant families find themselves torn by assimilationist commands, learn English, surrender ancient cultures, embrace U.S. material values. In the face of injustice one man rejects becoming a citizen, and another states he will "not come back to this country." Particularly among people of color, a rage smolders about heartless men, hard times and a bigoted fist that crushes their dreams.

Embedded in the anger is a bristling, defiant humanity, often individual and chaotic, but sometimes organized. Though these men and women lack economic security or legal status, many are ready to confront entrenched power. Some stand up to a patriarchal husband, an overbearing father, or society's inhibiting mores. Others flee oppressive bosses, confront racist tormentors, or escape from armed exploiters. Some raise their voices against the rich or their representatives, or contest control of the state by the few. They do not use words such as "daring," "bold," and "heroic," but they do resist those who would stifle their spirit or limit their lives.

A hundred years ago, these stories reveal, ordinary people gave of their skill, muscle, and energy to build a country that often ignored their contributions and scoffed at their suffering. Then, from within their souls, they summoned up extra measures of courage, ingenuity and challenge, and carried on.

These selections cover a spectrum of extraordinary lives found at the bottom of the U.S. pyramid at the turn of the century. A few have been edited to eliminate wordy asides and irrelevant wanderings, but every effort has been made to preserve the individual's focus, intent, and meaning.

The men and women whose lives unfold here represent an emerging America, rather than a complete portrait of the age. Nor should they be used as the era's sole source of information. But taken together these personal narratives—too long buried—represent an invaluable American legacy and an important resource for understanding a troubled time.

Mary: Keeping a Job,
Losing a Job

Factory work not only entailed long hours, grueling tasks, and inadequate wages, but often meant sudden joblessness for men and women employees. By the early twentieth century, women workers played a prominent role in unions and strikes. At thirty-four, "Mary" had worked all her life and looked ten years older. She was one of thirty women who had lost their jobs during a strike at a Fall River mill. Mary and the others came to Boston to seek work as domestic servants. There her story was taken down by Gertrude Barnum, National Secretary of the Women's Trade Union League, who characterized Mary as round-shouldered, nervous, and ane-

mic. "I can't write. I never got much schoolin'," Mary admitted, but her dictated story is clear-eyed, succinct, and a poignant reminder that the untutored have much to tell us about the past.

My mother, she was sick all the time. She worked in the mills in England since she was nine years. I had to stay at home and tend the children and help 'round ever since I was little. There were four younger'n me. I got a job 'spoolertender' when I was twelve—there wasn't the law then. I must have been about fourteen when I went to weavin' and I got them first four looms! I liked the mill better than workin' at home. At first the noise is fierce, and you have breathe the cotton all the time, but you get used to it. Lots of us is deaf—weavers—that's one reason I couldn't get that second girl place. The lady said I couldn't hear the door bell if it would ring, but you never think of the noise after the first, in the mill. Only it's bad one way: when the bobbins flies out and a girl gets hurt, you can't hear her shout—not if she just screams, you can't. She's got to wait 'till you see her. I saw a man hit with his mouth open. His teeth got knocked out and all the roof of his mouth tore. You can't never tell when you will get hit—in the eye some time, most likely!

We girls used to talk 'sign-talk'—with your mouth and fingers, you know—you can have lots of fun that way. We used to sit and crochet, even, right on the floor, betweens watchin' the looms. My mother, she was paralyzed two years before she died. She was awful heavy to lift. We couldn't get no insurance on her, of course. But we have got one hundred and thirty dollars in all on my father and me. It's hard payin' insurance every week. Some weeks you don't get off much cloth. Some weeks you only get two or three days' work, when they're 'curtailin'.' Like as not your mill will 'shut down' three months. We ain't got insurance for Ellen—she's next to me. She's twenty-eight now. Tom, he's got insurance for his own. His wife never worked since she got the first child. She never had no health. They lived with us, and he's got three children, and he's only twenty-four now. He is a good, sober worker, Tom is. The next brother he died when he was only two, and my other brother ain't much for the mills—he ain't much for no work. He never got no bringin'-up; he was 'boarded out' when he was little, and some of 'em gets like that. He goes away lookin' for work 'round in other towns, but he don't make out very well. He's twenty. Father, he is a 'slasher-tender,' but he ain't done much since ma died—and before, too—only more, after.

She stayed home so't I could work more steady. She ain't so very smart, but she is steady and she can make pretty good in the mills when she gets the work reg'lar. But she could only get 'sick weavin'' lots of the time (that's when some one is sick and you take her work till they get back. Lots of the girls has to 'ask out' reg'lar every month or so for a week. They can't stand it).

Ellen's kind of plain, and you know how it is—the good lookin' girls gets the best chance. Now there's French Charlie, he's one of the 'supers'—he never will take only pretty girls; he takes mostly French girls, too, of course. But French Charlie, he don't cheat you on your cloth; some 'supers' are terr'ble mean that way. You got to fight for your pay after you earn it, and like as not you'll miss a dollar.

If our family had all stuck together and joined a buildin' club, and Tom he hadn't got married, we could have owned a cottage by now, but we ain't as bad off as my uncle and aunt. They got a lot paid on their house and then they couldn't pay for a little while, and the landlord took it all off'n 'em—just like they never put up a cent. Some people makes lots of money that way. There's a man named Flint, one of the mill men; he just watches, and when you can't pay he puts you out, and keeps all the money, and then he gets some other people and fools 'em the same and—well, he makes more out of weavin', and that's a cinch.

We saved some, but somethin' always comes. Sickness is the worst. When you drive on eight looms all the time in busy season you get sort of 'spent,' and you catch cold easy. In winter they don't shovel off the paths half the time 'round them mills, and you got to go right out of the mill to your knees in snow. Then like as not you have to wait a long time in the snow for the freight trains to pass. Some of the girls take sick awful sudden and never get back for their pay envelopes—they go that quick sometimes. It was like that when you got so tired 'drivin''at eight looms, and when they gave us twelve looms I didn't see that we could make out to live at all. They talk about the electric stop makin' it easy. The girls say it's harder anyway with twelve looms and you don't make as much. We never seen no electric stops at our mill—just got four more straight looms. It makes you crazy watchin' 'em. You just try it! But that don't make no matter—there's plenty waitin' at the gates for our jobs, I guess. The Polaks learn weavin' quick, and they just as soon live on nothin' and work like that. But it won't do 'em much good for all they'll make out of it. They're welcome.

They say the mills is comin' down in wages 'til we get like in the South. Well, it is just as well to know about it, and then the smart ones will 'get through' and get a livin' out of somethin' else, it they can, and leave 'em to beat down the Portagee.

It's terrible in Fall River with the strike. You don't hear nothin' else. Every one's spent all they saved (some were good at savin'). You are owin' rent, and if you've 'got a store,' you've got that to pay, too—on nothin'—when the mills opens again. The union was good to us. My brother Tom, he's union. We didn't keep it up lately, Ellen and me, times was so hard. The union helped all they could. They gave us checks on the store sometimes and sometimes things from the farms. We used to get fish and berries when the season was. The Portagees was lucky—them as had the little vegetable gardens. The Salvation Army was good, too. They feed the children, you know. Tom's biggest girl hated to go, she'd rather go hungry; but they all came to it. They'd bring home soup and bread—and we got so we needed it bad. I guess that's about what my folks makes out on now—'the benefits' Tom gets and the soup and bread. We've got to get a place soon, Ellen and me, and send somethin' back.

Some of the girls that's workin' out in Boston, they ain't much struck on it. They say it's terrible lonesome. You ain't as good as the people you live with, and you get terrible long hours—you're just never through. Your 'day out' means pretty near four o'clock in the afternoon before you get to go, and you got no place to go much when you do get out—so far away from every one. 'Taint like Fall River, where you know people. I don't see as there is much hope unless the unions get us up some way. I kind of hate to leave the mills. I worked there all my life. Do you think you can get me and Ellen a place together?

Ross B. Moudy: Clashing
Values in Colorado's Mines

At the turn of the century, workers and employers often found themselves engaged in battle, as bosses sought to maximize profits, and laborers demanded a living wage and safe working conditions. Few rules governed the work place, even fewer were enforced, and capitalists counted on sympathetic judges, legislators, and governors to take their side in any dispute with employees.

Ross B. Moudy, who came to work at a Cripple Creek mine in Colorado, provides a vivid picture of the turmoil and violence generated by the mine industry's contending protagonists: stockholders, bosses, scabs, and union and non-union workers.

Before I went to Cripple Creek I went to work in a chlori-
nation mill in Florence, which is just thirty miles south of
Cripple Creek, and found that I had arrived just in time
to reap the benefit of a strike there, which the mill workers had won the day before. It seems that they had been
working nine and ten hours a day for from $1.50 to $2.00
per day, and as one could not get board and room anywhere for less than $30.00 per month, it took just about
all one could earn to live on, especially as the mill would
shut down for at least two days every month and two percent of the wages were deducted for hospital fees. The work
in the mill is not so dangerous as disagreeable and un-
healthy, as one is all the time in an atmosphere of sulphur
dioxide, or chlorin, or dust, so that one cannot see an object
two feet away; so it was no wonder to me that they struck.
But $2.00 for eight hours of that kind of work is nothing
great.

It was not long before the dust and gas began to act on
me and I went to the mill surgeon about it. He told me I
had better quit, but asked me not to tell the managers, for
they always had a hard time to fill those places, and that
no man could stand it long. So I quit and went to Cripple
Creek.

The minimum wages for miners and men working
around the mines at Cripple Creek was $3.00 per day. Men
running machine drills got from $4.00 to $6.00 per day,
according to the kind of place they had to work in—that
is, whether the place was wet or dangerous. Machine men
working in a wet shaft usually got about $6.00, and the
helpers got from 50 cents to $1.00 less than the machine

men. Engineers received from $4.00 to $7.00 a day, depending on the place they worked in.

In all the mines around Cripple Creek the miners worked only eight hours a day, and on a good many mines the miners were allowed to go down in the mine, come out of the mine, eat dinner and change clothes on the company's time. That means, that if the men begin to go down into the holes at 8 a.m., come out at 11:30 and eat dinner, go down again at noon, begin to come out sometimes as early as twenty minutes to four and change clothes, and at 4 p.m. they can go; so they do not all of them work eight hours, but often times nearer seven hours. Of course, most of the mines worked the men the full eight hours.

The last mine in which I worked was a very safe mine compared with most of them, but the dangers do not seem so great to a practiced miner, who is used to climbing hundreds of feet on stulls or braces put about six feet apart, one above the other, and then walking the same distance on a couple of poles sometimes not larger than fence rails, where a misstep would mean a long drop. But to a novice all the dangers stand out doubly strong. For instance, the stockholders of the mine I worked at visited the mine in a body. They were wealthy capitalists from New York, Boston and Chicago. Well, the first thing they did was to get inside the bucket, because they dared not stand on the rim and hold to the cable to ride down as the miners do. One of the capitalists in particular seemed to be afraid even to walk on the solid rock of the bottom level, and when the superintendent finally succeeded in getting him up into one of the stopes after a series of falls and slips he looked more like a ghost than a man. He told one of the miners, who was working near him, that he thought it took lots of courage to work in a place like that, and when the miner told him that they got used to it, he said that instead of being paid $3.00 per day they ought to have all the gold they could take out.

The hospital discount is usually from one to two dollars a month, and merely gives one attendance if he is hurt. This is deducted from your check every month. On some mines it is compulsory to take this. This is not admitted by the managers, but the unions have watched it pretty carefully, and if a man does not pay hospital fees he does not stay very long at his job. The same thing is true of the mine insurance, which is from three to five dollars a month. This insurance is put up by some of the insurance companies, and, of course, as they do not have to have an agent to collect this money every month, it is supposed that the management gets a rake-off. But the worst of it is that if a man is hurt badly or disabled for life through the carelessness of the mine's managers, before he receives his insurance he has to sign a paper releasing the mine owners from all responsibility for the accident, and then he cannot collect damages in the courts. In this way the mine owners shield themselves against the consequences of their neglect of the legal precautions for the safety of the men. The managers say that they have this insurance as a help for the men, as some of them would not have a cent if they were killed and leave large families, but on some of the mines, even if a man had insurance in a good company and did not want to, or could not afford to, take out more, he has the mine insurance forced on him against his will, and at higher premium than he would have to pay to an independent company. In Cripple Creek there are no company stores, and the miners do not have to furnish their own powder when they work for wages.

While I was in Cripple Creek there was only one mine, the "Strong," which would not employ union men, and a number of them would employ nothing but union men, and every month the men would have to show their union card paid up; but at most of the mines it made no difference whether a man was union or non-union, just as long as his work was satisfactory.

Shortly after I went to Cripple Creek the union posted notices that all men working in mines would have to join the union by a certain date, or be called a scab, and the walking delegate came to me and told me if I did not join I could not work at the mines. If he had asked me to join I would probably have done it, but as it was, I didn't join for a year when a friend of mine presented the matter in a favorable light.

There were a few fights and deeds of violence after the date set for joining the union, but they subsided, and one seemed just as safe whether he was union or non-union. Up to the time I joined I was acquainted with a number of very nice men who belonged to the union, and most of the union men I met did not treat me any differently than they did members. I joined because I saw it would help me to keep in work and for protection in case of accident or sickness, for the union is just like any other secret order that way. They pay ten dollars a week sick benefits, and hire three nurses at three dollars per day of eight hours; so if one is alone and sick he is sure to be taken care of. There were a good many mines where they required union men, and as I was out of work a good deal I found out that it was easier to get work and keep work on those mines if I had a union card.

Of course, there were a lot of hotheads in the union, but they were always held down, and I know from attending the union meetings during one strike down there that they never talked dynamite before the union as a whole, for the union leaders kept cautioning against such things as likely to hurt their cause. But there are some men who are always ready to take matters in their own hands and do what they think is best with violence.

The president and the secretary of the union I belonged to were both young men, who were leasing a mine and hiring men themselves and were making quite a stake, but they held on to the union; and when a strike was called they would not even ship their own ore, because it would go to a non-union mill, so they stopped work until they could get a union mill to treat their ore for them. This was the time when the strike was first started in sympathy with the mill in Colorado Springs and Colorado City.

While I was in Cripple Creek about a dozen Austrians came up from the coal camps and were going to do cheap labor; so a bunch of men escorted them out of town and told them not to come back; but these men were not all union men, for even non-union men like to draw their three and three and a half dollars a day. So now the Citizens' Alliance claim that they can do the same thing as well as the union men; but, of course, two wrongs do not make a right, and, besides, they have gone into places and destroyed property which belonged to the union. Of course, they are in power, as they have their own organization backed by the militia, but the camp will be unionized again some time, for the men will not work without trying to protect themselves against accidents in the dangerous places where they have to work, in such mantraps as the "Hoosier" mine, for instance.

The mining laws of Colorado are not enforced at all, and it is on account of this that so many lives are lost. The mine inspector very seldom goes to Cripple Creek, and, when he does, he does not stay more than a few days, and, of course, cannot see one hundredth part of the mines. If he should make an inspection of a single one of the big mines it would take all the time he usually spends in the entire district.

For example, the mining laws of Colorado require a cage for every shaft over two hundred feet deep, and I do not know one hole two hundred feet deep that has a cage, and know of lots that are from four to six hundred that have nothing but a bucket. Things like these an inspector would not have to go down in a mine at all to find out.

Then, too, many of the mines have immense stopes with hardly a timber in them, and these places are known all over the camp, but the mine inspector seems never to find it out. In short, the mine inspection in Cripple Creek is nothing but a farce.

A good point about the unions is the attention they give to the State Government. Every bill that passes the Legislature or that is presented to the Legislature is read in the union and discussed, and if they are not satisfactory to the union they call upon their representatives to work against it. Most of the union men are socialists, but they believe the change will come about gradually and not by revolution.

The part of mining that bothered me the most was the mine gas, owing to poor ventilation, and many times I have been carried out unconscious and not able to work for two or three days after. Several men died from effects of gas while I was in the district. But outside of getting a couple of toes smashed from falling rocks and a crack on the head from a bolt which fell about two hundred feet down the shaft and struck the door and glanced into the station, knocking me out for over a week, I got out of the district rather luckily.

I batched for the last year I was in Cripple Creek, as I found I could save a little money that way. The house I lived in was made of one thickness of boards, covered with corrugated iron—an oven in summer and an ice-box in winter. I had to get up early in the morning, eat my breakfast half cooked and half frozen, and then walk, or run, a mile and a half over the trail to the mine. A man changes every two weeks to another of the three eight-hour shifts into which the day is divided. After I got back to the shack and got cleaned up and my supper cooked and eaten, it was usually too late and I was too tired to do anything more than read the paper, or write a letter home or to the one who would soon make a home for me.

A Farming Woman:
Expanding Horizons

Americans have always celebrated those who work close to the soil as being "close to God." The man who produces the nation's crops has been a hero to generations, a sturdy bulwark of morality, hard work, and stamina. Yet farmers' wives have rarely received their due. They worked alongside their husbands in the field and then returned to take care of home and children. They too helped build a nation and seldom had time to enjoy the fruits of their labors.

How heavy their load really was and how they felt about it has often escaped attention. That is why this autobiography of an anonymous woman is so instructive. Her work schedule, incredibly burdensome, monotonous, and unending, was typical. And despite her enormous contribution to the success of the farm, her part of the marital relationship required her to dutifully accept her husband's commands, no matter how strongly opposed her own inclinations might be.

I have been a farmer's wife in one of the states of the Middle West for thirteen years, and everybody knows that the farmer's wife must of a necessity be a very practical woman, if she would be a successful one.

I am not a practical woman and consequently have been accounted a failure by practical friends and especially by my husband, who is wholly practical.

We are told that the mating of people of opposite natures promotes intellectuality in the offspring; but I think that happy homes are of more consequence than extreme precocity of children. However, I believe that people who are thinking of mating do not even consider whether it is to be the one or the other.

We do know that when people of opposite tastes get married, there's a discordant note that runs through their married life. It's only a question of which taste shall predominate.

In our case my husband had the stronger will; he is innocent of book learning, is a natural hustler who believes that the only way to make an honest living lies in digging it out of the ground, so to speak, and being a farmer, he finds plenty of digging to do; he has an inherited tendency to be miserly, loves money for its own sake rather than for its purchasing power, and when he has it in his possession he is loath to part with it, even for the most necessary articles, and prefers to eschew hired help in every possible instance that what he does make may be his very own.

No man can run a farm without someone to help him, and in this case I have always been called upon and expected to help do anything that a man would be expected to do; I began this when we were first married, when there were few household duties and no reasonable excuse for refusing to help.

I was reared on a farm, was healthy and strong, was ambitious, and the work was not disagreeable, and having no children for the first six years of married life, the habit of going whenever asked to became firmly fixed, and he had no thought of hiring a man to help him, since I could do anything for which he needed help.

I was an apt student at school and before I was eighteen I had earned a teacher's certificate of the second grade and would gladly have remained in school a few more years, but I had, unwittingly, agreed to marry the man who is now my husband, and tho I begged to be released, his will was so much the stronger that I was unable to free myself without wounding a loving heart, and could not find it in my heart to do so.

All through life I have found my dislike for giving offense to be my undoing. When we were married and moved away from my home church, I fain would have adopted the church of my new residence, but my husband did not like to go to church; had rather go visiting on Sundays, and, rather than have my right hand give offense, I cut it off.

I always had a passion for reading; during girlhood it was along educational lines; in young womanhood it was for love stories, which remained ungratified because my father thought it sinful to read stories of any kind, and especially love stories.

Later, when I was married, I borrowed everything I could find in the line of novels and stories, and read them by stealth still, for my husband thought it a willful waste of time to read anything and that it showed a lack of love for him if I would rather read than to talk to him when I had a few moments of leisure, and in order to avoid giving offense and still gratify my desire, I would only read when he was not at the house, thereby greatly curtailing my already too limited reading hours.

In reading miscellaneously I got glimpses now and then of the great poets and authors, which aroused a great desire for a thorough perusal of them all; but up till the present time I have not been permitted to satisfy this desire. As the years have rolled on, there has been more work and less leisure until it is only by the greatest effort that I may read current news.

It is only during the last three years that I have had the news to read, for my husband is so very penurious that he would never consent to subscribing for papers of any kind, and that old habit of avoiding that which would give offense was so fixed that I did not dare to break it.

The addition of two children to our family never altered or interfered with the established order of things to any appreciable extent. My strenuous outdoor life agreed with me, and even when my children were born, I was splendidly prepared for the ordeal and made rapid recovery. I still hoed and tended the truck patches and garden, still watered the stock and put out feed for them, still went to the hay field and helped harvest and house the bounteous crops;

still helped harvest the golden grain later on when the cereals ripened; often took one team and dragged ground to prepare the seedbed for wheat for weeks at a time, while my husband was using the other team on another farm which he owns several miles away.

While the children were babies, they were left at the house, and when they were larger, they would go with me to my work; now they are large enough to help a little during the summer and to go to school in winter; they help a great deal during the fruit canning season—in fact, they can and do work at almost everything, pretty much as I do.

All the season, from the coming in of the first fruits until the making of mincemeat at Christmastime, I put up canned goods for future use; gather in many bushels of field beans and the other crops usually raised on the farm; make sauerkraut, ketchup, pickles, etc.

This is a vague, general idea of how I spend my time; my work is so varied that it would be difficult, indeed, to describe a typical day's work.

Any bright morning in the latter part of May I am out of bed at four o'clock; next, after I have dressed and combed my hair, I start a fire in the kitchen stove, and while the stove is getting hot I go to my flower garden and gather a choice, half-blown rose and a spray of bride's wreath and arrange them in my hair, and sweep the floors and then cook breakfast.

While the other members of the family are eating breakfast, I strain away the morning's milk (for my husband milks the cows while I get breakfast) and fill my husband's dinner-pail, for he will go to work on our other farm for the day.

By this time it is half-past five o'clock, my husband is gone to his work, and the stock loudly pleading to be turned into the pastures. The younger cattle, a half dozen steers, are left in the pasture at night, and I now drive the two cows a half-quarter mile and turn them in with the others, come back, and then there's a horse in the barn that belongs in a field where there is no water, which I take to a spring quite a distance from the barn; bring it back and turn it into a field with the sheep, a dozen in number, which are housed at night.

The young calves are then turned out into the warm sunshine, and the stock hogs, which are kept in a pen, are clamoring for food, and I carry a pailful of swill to them, and hasten to the house and turn out the chickens and put out feed and water for them, and it is, perhaps, *6:30* a.m.

I have not eaten breakfast yet, but that can wait; I make the beds next and straighten things up in the living room, for I dislike to have the early morning caller find my house topsy-turvy. When this is done I go to the kitchen, which also serves as a dining room, and uncover the table, and take a mouthful of food occasionally as I pass to and fro at my work until my appetite is appeased.

By the time the work is done in the kitchen it is about *7:15* a.m., and the cool morning hours have flown, and no hoeing done in the garden yet, and the children's toilet has to be attended to and churning has to be done.

Finally the children are washed and churning done, and it is eight o'clock, and the sun getting hot, but no matter, weeds die quickly when cut down in the heat of the day, and I use the hoe to a good advantage until the dinner hour, which is *11:30* a.m. We come in, and I comb my hair, and put out feed and water for the chickens; set a hen, perhaps, sweep the floors again; sit down and rest, and read a few moments, and it is nearly one o'clock, and I sweep the door yard while I am waiting for the clock to strike the hour.

I make and sow a flower bed, dig around some shrubbery, and go back to the garden to hoe until time to do the chores at night, but ere long some hogs come up to the back gate, through the wheat field, and when I go to see what is wrong I find that the cows have torn the fence down, and they too, are in the wheat field.

With much difficulty I get them back into their own domain and repair the fence. I hoe in the garden till four o'clock; then I go into the house and get supper, and prepare something for the dinner-pail tomorrow; when supper is all ready it is set aside, and I pull a few hundred plants of tomato, sweet potato or cabbage for transplanting, set them in a cool, moist place where they will not wilt, and I then go after the horse, water him, and put him in the barn; call the sheep and house them, and go after the cows and milk them, feed the hogs, put down hay for three horses, and put oats and corn in their troughs, and set those plants and come in and fasten up the chickens, and it is dark. By this time it is 8 o'clock p.m.; my husband has come home, and we are eating supper; when we are through eating I make the beds ready, and the children and their father go to bed, and I wash the dishes and get things in shape to get breakfast quickly next morning.

It is now about 9 o'clock p.m., and after a short prayer I retire for the night.

As a matter of course, there's hardly two days together which require the same routine, yet every day is as fully occupied in some way or other as this one, with varying tasks as the seasons change. In early spring we are planting potatoes, making plant beds, planting garden, early corn patches, setting strawberries, planting corn, melons, cow peas, sugar cane, beans, popcorn, peanuts, etc.

Oats are sown in March and April, but I do not help do this, because the ground is too cold.

Later in June we harvest clover hay, in July timothy hay, and in August pea hay.

Winter wheat is ready to harvest the latter part of June, and oats the middle of July.

These are the main crops, supplemented by cabbages, melons, potatoes, tomatoes, etc.

Fully half of my time is devoted to helping my husband, more than half during the active work season, and not that much during the winter months; only a very small portion of my time is devoted to reading. My reading matter accumulates during the week, and I think I will stay at home on Sunday and read, but as we have many visitors on Sunday I am generally disappointed.

I sometimes visit my friends on Sunday because they are so insistent that I should, tho I would prefer spending the day reading quietly at home. I have never had a vacation, but if I should be allowed one I should certainly be pleased to spend it in an art gallery.

As winter draws nigh I make snug all the vegetables and apples, pumpkins, and such things as would damage by being frozen, and gather in the various kinds of nuts which grow in our woods, to eat during the long, cold winter.

My husband's work keeps him away from home during the day all the winter, except in extremely inclement weather, and I feed and water the stock, which have been brought in off the pastures; milk the cows and do all the chores which are to be done about a farm in winter.

A Farming Woman

By getting up early and hustling around pretty lively I do all this and countless other things; keep house in a crude, simple manner; wash, make, and mend our clothes; make rag carpets, cultivate and keep more flowers than anybody in the neighborhood, raise some chickens to sell and some to keep, and even teach instrumental music sometimes.

I have always had an itching to write, and with all my multitudinous cares, I have written, in a fitful way, for several papers, which do not pay for such matter, just because I was pleased to see my articles in print.

I have a long list of correspondents, who write regularly and often to me, and, by hook and crook, I keep up with my letter-writing, for, next to reading, I love to write and receive letters, tho my husband says I will break him up buying so much writing material; when, as a matter of course, I pay for it out of my own scanty income.

I am proud of my children, and have, from the time they were young babies, tried to make model children of them. They were not spoiled as some babies are, and their education was begun when I first began to speak to them, with the idea of not having the work to do over later on. True, they did not learn to spell until they were old enough to start to school, because I did not have time to teach them that; but, in going about my work, I told them stories of all kinds, in plain, simple language which they could understand, and after once hearing a story they could repeat it in their own way, which did not differ greatly form mine, to anyone who cared to listen, for they were not timid or afraid of anybody.

I have watched them closely, and never have missed an opportunity to correct their errors until their language is as correct as that of the average adult, as far as their vocabulary goes, and I have tried to make it as exhaustive as my time would permit.

I must admit that there is very little time for the higher life for myself, but my soul cries out for it, and my heart is not in my homely duties; they are done in a mechanical, abstracted way, not worthy of a woman of high ambitions; but my ambitions are along other lines.

I do not mean to say that I have no ambition to do my work well, and to be a model housekeeper, for I would scorn to slight my work intentionally; it is just this way: There are so many outdoor duties that the time left for house-hold duties is so limited that I must rush through them, with a view to getting each one done in the shortest pos-sible time, in order to get as many things accomplished as possible, for there is never time to do half as much as needs to be done.

All the time that I have been going about this work I have been thinking of things I have read; of things I have on hand to read when I can get time, and of other things which I have a desire to read, but cannot hope to while the present condition exists.

As a natural consequence, there are, daily, numerous instances of absent-mindedness on my part; many things left undone that I really could have done, by leaving off something else of less importance, if I had not forgotten the thing of the more importance. My husband never fails to remind me that it is caused by my reading so much; that I would get along much better if I should never see a book or paper, while really I would be distracted if all reading matter was taken from me.

I use an old-fashioned churn, and the process of churning occupies from thirty minutes to three hours, according to the condition of the cream, and I always read something while churning, and tho that may look like a poor way to attain self-culture, yet if your reading is of the nature to bring about that desirable result, one will surely be greatly benefited by these daily exercises.

But if one is just reading for amusement, they might read a great deal more than that and not derive any benefit; but my reading has always been for the purpose of becoming well informed; and when knitting stockings for the family I always have a book or paper in reading distance; or, if I have a moment to rest or to wait on something, I pick up something and read during the time. I even take a paper with me to the fields and read while I stop for rest.

I often hear ladies remark that they do not have time to read. I happen to know that they have a great deal more time than I do, but not having any burning desire to read, the time is spent in some other way; often spent at a neighbor's house gossiping about the other neighbors.

I suppose it is impossible for a woman to do her best at everything that she would like to do, but I really would like to. I almost cut sleep out of my routine in trying to keep up all the rows which I have started in on; in the short winter days I just get the cooking and house straightening done in addition to looking after the stock and poultry, and make a garment occasionally, and wash and iron the clothes; all the other work is done after night by lamplight, and when the work for the day is over, or at least the most pressing part of it, and the family are all asleep and no one to forbid it, I spend a few hours writing or reading.

The minister who performed the marriage ceremony for us has always taken a kindly interest in our fortunes and, knowing of my literary bent, has urged me to turn it to account; but there seemed to be so little time and opportunity that I could not think seriously of it, altho I longed for a literary career; but my education had been dropped for a dozen years or more, and I knew that I was not properly equipped for that kind of a venture.

This friend was so insistent that I was induced to compete for a prize in a short story contest in a popular magazine not long since, tho I entered it fully prepared for a failure.

About that time there came in my way the literature of a correspondence school which would teach, among other things, short story writing by mail. The school has proven very trustworthy, and I am in the midst of a course of instruction which is very pleasing to me; and I find time for study and exercise between the hours of eight and eleven at night, when the family are asleep and quiet. I am instructed to read a great deal, with a certain purpose in view, but that is impossible, since I had to promise my husband that I would drop all my papers, periodicals, etc., on which I was paying out money for subscription before he would consent to my taking the course. This I felt willing to do, that I might prepare myself for more congenial tasks; I hope to accomplish something worthy of note in a literary way since I have been a failure in all other pursuits.

My friends have always been so kind as not to hint that I had not come up to their expectations in various lines, but I inwardly knew that they regarded me as a financial failure; they knew that my husband would not allow the money that was made off the farm to be spent on the family, but still they knew of other men who did the same, yet the wives managed some way to have money of their own and to keep up the family expenses and clothe themselves and children nicely anyhow, but they did not seem to take into account that these thrifty wives had the time all for their own in which to earn a livelihood while my time was demanded by my husband, to be spent in doing things for him which would add nothing to my income, since I was supposed to look to my own resources for my spending money.

When critical housewives spend the day with me I always feel that my surroundings appear to a disadvantage. They cannot possibly know the inside working of our home, and knowing myself to be capable of the proper management of a home if I had the chance of others, I feel like I am receiving a mental criticism from them which is unmerited, and when these smart neighbors tell me proudly how many young chicks they have, and how many eggs and old hens they have sold during the year, I am made to feel that they are crowing over their shrewdness, which they regard as lacking in me, because they will persist in measuring my opportunities by their own.

I might add that the neighbors among whom I live are illiterate and unmusical, and that my redeeming qualities, in their eyes, are my superior education and musical abilities; they are kind enough to give me more than justice on these qualities because they are poor judges of such matters.

But money is king, and if I might turn my literary bent to account, and surround myself with the evidences of prosperity, I may yet hope fully to redeem myself in their eyes, and I know that I will have attained my ambition in that line.

Rose Schneiderman:
Becoming a Union
Organizer

A short, energetic, determined young Jewish immigrant, Rose Schneiderman began her career in the United States working in a New York City hat factory. Once she saw that the women she labored alongside needed to be organized, she devoted her long life to promoting unionism. She later became a feminist, the Secretary of the New York Department of Labor, and an internationally known advocate of trade unions.

In 1905, when Schneiderman's autobiographical essay appeared, she was only twenty-one; her ideas had not fully formed, but she had enthusiastically thrown herself headlong into her first union campaign.

Rose Schneiderman

My name is Rose Schneiderman, and I was born in some small city of Russian Poland. I don't know the name of the city, and have no memory of that part of my childhood. When I was about five years of age my parents brought me to this country and we settled in New York.

So my earliest recollections are of living in a crowded street among the East Side Jews, for we also are Jews.

My father got work as a tailor, and we lived in two rooms on Eldridge Street, and did very well, though not so well as in Russia, because mother and father both earned money, and here father alone earned the money, while mother attended to the house. There were then two other children besides me, a boy of three and one of five.

I went to school until I was nine years old, enjoying it thoroughly and making great progress, but then my father died of brain fever and mother was left with three children and another one coming. So I had to stay at home to help her and she went out to look for work.

A month later the baby was born, and mother got work in a fur house, earning about $6 a week and afterward $8 a week, for she was clever and steady.

I was the house worker, preparing the meals and looking after the other children—the baby, a little girl of six years, and a boy of nine. I managed very well, though the meals were not very elaborate. I could cook simple things like porridge, coffee and eggs, and mother used to prepare the meat before she went away in the morning, so that all I had to do was to put it in the pan at night.

The children were not more troublesome than others, but this was a hard part of my life with few bright spots in it. I was a serious child, and cared little for children's play, and I knew nothing about the country, so it was not so bad for me as it might have been for another. Yet it was bad, though I did get some pleasure from reading, of which I was very fond; and now and then, as a change from the home, I took a walk in the crowded street.

Mother was absent from half-past seven o'clock in the morning till half-past six o'clock in the evening.

I was finally released by my little sister being taken by an aunt, and the two boys going to the Hebrew Orphan Asylum, which is a splendid institution, and turns out good men. One of these brothers is now a student in the City College, and the other is a page in the Stock Exchange.

When the other children were sent away mother was able to send me back to school, and I stayed in this school (Houston Street Grammar) till I had reached the Sixth Grammar Grade.

Then I had to leave in order to help support the family. I got a place in Hearn's as cash girl, and after working there three weeks changed to Ridley's, where I remained for two and a half years. I finally left because the pay was so very poor and there did not seem to be any chance of advancement, and a friend told me that I could do better making caps.

So I got a place in the factory of Hein & Fox. The hours were from 8 a.m. to 6 p.m., and we made all sorts of linings—or, rather, we stitched in the linings—golf caps, yachting caps, etc. It was piece work, and we received from 3½ cents to 10 cents a dozen, according to the different grades. By working hard we could make an average of about $5 a week. We would have made more but had to provide our own machines, which cost us $45, we paying for them on the installment plan. We paid $5 down and $1 a month after that.

I learned the business in about two months, and then made as much as the others, and was consequently doing quite well when the factory burned down, destroying all our machines—150 of them. This was very hard on the girls who had paid for their machines. It was not so bad for me, as I had only paid a little of what I owed.

The bosses got $500,000 insurance, so I heard, but they never gave the girls a cent to help them bear their losses. I think they might have given them $10, anyway.

Soon work went on again in four lofts, and a little later I became assistant sample maker. This is a position which, though coveted by many, pays better in glory than in cash. It was still piece work, and though the pay per dozen was better the work demanded was of a higher quality, and one could not rush through samples as through the other caps. So I still could average only about $5 per week.

After I had been working as a cap maker for three years it began to dawn on me that we girls needed an organization. The men had organized already, and had gained some advantages, but the bosses had lost nothing, as they took it out of us.

We were helpless; no one girl dare stand up for anything alone. Matters kept getting worse. The bosses kept making reductions in our pay, half a cent a dozen at a time. It did not sound important, but at the end of the week we found a difference.

We didn't complain to the bosses; we didn't say anything except to each other. There was no use. The bosses would not pay any attention unless we were like the men and could make them attend.

One girl would say that she didn't think she could make caps for the new price, but another would say that she thought she could make up for the reduction by working a little harder, and then the first would tell herself:

"If she can do it, why can't I?"

They didn't think how they were wasting their strength.

A new girl from another shop got in among us. She was Miss Bessie Brout, and she talked organization as a remedy for our ills. She was radical and progressive, and she stimulated thoughts which were already in our minds before she came.

Finally Miss Brout and I and another girl went to the National Board of United Cloth Hat and Cap Makers when it was in session, and asked them to organize the girls.

They asked us:

"How many of you are there willing to be organized?"

"In the first place about twelve," we said. We argued that the union label would force the bosses to organize their girls, and if there was a girls' union in existence the bosses could not use the union label unless their girls belonged to the union.

We were told to come to the next meeting of the National Board, which we did, and then received a favorable answer, and were asked to bring all the girls who were willing to be organized to the next meeting, and at the next meeting, accordingly, we were there twelve strong and were organized.

When Fox found out what had happened he discharged Miss Brout, and probably would have discharged me but that I was a sample maker and not so easy to replace. In a few weeks we had all the girls in the organization, because the men told the girls that they must enter the union or they would not be allowed to work in the shop.

Then came a big strike. Price lists for the coming season were given in to the bosses, to which they did not agree. After some wrangling a strike was declared in five of the biggest factories. There are 30 factories in the city. About 100 girls went out.

The result was a victory, which netted us—I mean the girls—$2 increase in our wages on the average.

All the time our union was progressing very nicely. There were lectures to make us understand what trades unionism is and our real position in the labor movement. I read upon the subject and grew more and more interested, and after a time I became a member of the National Board, and had duties and responsibilities that kept me busy after my day's work was done.

But all was not lovely by any means, for the bosses were not at all pleased with their beating and had determined to fight us again.

They agreed among themselves that after the 26th of December, 1904, they would run their shops on the "open" system.

This agreement was reached last fall, and soon notices, reading as follows, were hung in the various shops:

NOTICE

After the 26th of December, 1904, this shop will be run on the open shop system, the bosses having the right to engage and discharge employees as they see fit, whether the latter are union or nonunion.

Of course, we knew that this meant an attack on the union. The bosses intended gradually to get rid of us, employing in our place child labor and raw immigrant girls who would work for next to nothing.

On December 22d the above notice appeared, and the National Board, which had known about it all along, went into session prepared for action.

Our people were very restive, saying that they could not sit under that notice, and that if the National Board did not call them out soon they would go out of themselves.

At last word was sent out, and at 2:30 o'clock all the workers stopped, and laying down their scissors and other tools, marched out, some of them singing the "Marseillaise."

We were out for thirteen weeks, and the girls established their reputation. They were on picket duty from seven o'clock in the morning till six o'clock in the evening, and gained over many of the nonunion workers by appeals to them to quit working against us.

Our theory was that if properly approached and talked to few would be found who would resist our offer to take them into our organization. No right thinking person desires to injure another. We did not believe in violence and never employed it.

During this strike period we girls each received $3 a week; single men $3 a week, and married men $5 a week. This was paid us by the National Board.

We were greatly helped by the other unions, because the open shop issue was a tremendous one, and this was the second fight which the bosses had conducted for it.

Their first was with the tailors, whom they beat. If they now could beat us the outlook for unionism would be bad.

Some were aided and we stuck [it] out, and won a glorious victory all along the line. That was only last week.

The shops are open now for all union hands and for them only.

While the strike lasted I tried to get work in a factory that was not affected, but found that the boss was against me.

Last spring I had gone as a member of a committee to appeal to this boss on behalf of a girl who had been four years in his employ and was only getting $7 a week. She wanted $1 raise and all legal holidays. Previously she had had to work on holidays. After argument we secured for her the $1 raise and half a day on every legal holiday.

When the strike broke out, looking for work, I went to this boss, and he stared at me, and said:

"What do you want?"

"You asked for a girl."

"You—you—I don't want you," said he. "Can't I have my choice?"

"Certainly," said I, "I could never work where I'm not wanted."

I suppose he expected me to revenge myself by keeping other girls away, but I sent him others till he filled the place.

He resented my having served on the committee, and so he did not want me, but I felt honored by the manner in which I was treated. It showed that I had done my duty.

The bosses try to represent this open shop issue as though they were fighting a battle for the public, but really it is nothing of the sort. The open shop is a weapon to break the unions and set men once more cutting each other's throats by individual competition.

Why, there was a time in the cap trade when men worked fourteen hours a day, and then took the heads of their machines home in bags and setting them up on stands, put mattresses underneath to deaden the sound and worked away till far into the morning.

We don't want such slavery as that to come back.

The shops are open now for all union people, and all nonunion people can join the union. In order to take in newcome foreigners we have for them cut the initiation fees down to one-half what we Americans have to pay, and we trust them till they get work and their wages.

In order to give the newcomers a chance we have stopped night work, which doesn't suit the bosses, because it causes them to pay more rent when they can't use their buildings night and day. It costs them the price of another loft instead of costing the workers their health and lives as in the old days.

Our trade is well organized, we have won two victories and are not going backward.

But there is much to be done in other directions. The shop girls certainly need organization, and I think that they ought to be easy to organize, as their duties are simple and regular and they have a regular scale of wages.

Many saleswomen on Grand and Division streets, and, in fact, all over the East Side, work from 8 a.m. till 9 p.m. week days, and one-half a day on Sundays for $5 and $6 a week; so they certainly need organization.

The waitresses also could easily be organized, and perhaps the domestic servants. I don't know about stenographers. I have not come in contact with them.

Women have proved in the late strike that they can be faithful to an organization and to each other. The men give us the credit of winning the strike.

Certainly our organization constantly grows stronger, and the Woman's Trade Union League makes progress.

Rose Schneiderman

The girls and women by their meetings and discussions come to understand and sympathize with each other, and more and more easily they act together.

It is the only way in which they can hope to hold what they now have or better present conditions.

Certainly there is no hope from the mercy of the bosses.

Each boss does the best he can for himself with no thought of the other bosses, and that compels each to gouge and squeeze his hands to the last penny in order to make a profit.

So we must stand together to resist, for we will get what we can take—just that and no more.

Lee Chew:
Fighting Discrimination

From the time the Chinese began to come to America in large numbers during the California Gold Rush in 1849, they were viewed with suspicion and treated with hostility. The majority of those who came were single males. Many originally intended to stay only until they made enough money to return home with some savings, and they did not surrender their own culture.

Their readiness to work hard for low pay—first demonstrated on the transcontinental railroad during the Civil War—made them the targets of white workingmen who resented them as job competitors. In 1882, Chinese were denied entrance to the United States. By the close of the nine-

teenth century, the Chinese had been shunned by labor unions, confined in ghettos, and attacked by mobs. They survived, however, because of strong family ties and a proud cultural tradition that viewed hostility from the outside as proof of their own superiority.

Most Chinese in America, unlike Lee Chew, were not successful storekeepers but menials, day laborers, and workers in the Chinese ghetto. Chew's castigation of Americans under his own signature represents no little courage for the Chinese American of his day. His attack on other immigrant groups was typical of those who faced persecution in America and suspected that others had it easier.

The village where I was born is situated in the province of Canton, on one of the banks of the Si-Kiang River. All in the village belonged to the tribe of Lee. They did not intermarry with one another, but the men went to other villages for their wives and brought them home to their fathers' houses, and men from other villages—Wus and Wings and Sings and Fongs, etc.—chose wives from among our girls.

When I was a baby I was kept in our house all the time with my mother, but when I was a boy of seven I had to sleep at nights with other boys of the village—about thirty of them in one house. The girls are separated the same way—thirty or forty of them sleeping together in one house away from their parents—and the widows have houses where they work and sleep, tho they go to their fathers' houses to eat.

In spite of the fact that any man may correct them for

a fault, Chinese boys have good times and plenty of play. We played games like tag, and other games like shinny and a sort of football called yin.

It was not all play for us boys, however. We had to go to school, where we learned to read and write and to recite the precepts of Kong-foo-tsze and the other Sages, and stories about the great emperors of China, who ruled with the wisdom of gods and gave to the whole world the light of high civilization and the culture of our literature, which is the admiration of all nations.

I went to my parents' house for meals, approaching my grandfather with awe, my father and mother with veneration, and my elder brother with respect. I worked on my father's farm till I was about sixteen years of age, when a man of our tribe came back from America and took ground as large as four city blocks and made a paradise of it. He put a large stone wall around and led some streams through and built a palace and summer house and about twenty other structures, with beautiful bridges over the streams and walks and roads. Trees and flowers, singing birds, waterfowl, and curious animals were within his walls.

The man had gone away from our village a poor boy. Now he returned with unlimited wealth, which he had obtained in the country of the American wizards. After many amazing adventures he had become a merchant in a city called Mott Street, so it was said.

The wealth of this man filled my mind with the idea that I, too, would like to go to the country of the wizards and gain some of their wealth, and after a long time my father consented, and gave me his blessing, and my mother took leave of me with tears, while my grandfather laid his hand upon my head and told me to remember and live up to the admonitions of the Sages, to avoid gambling, bad women, and men of evil minds, and so to govern my conduct that when I died my ancestors might rejoice to welcome me as a guest on high.

My father gave me $100, and I went to Hong Kong with five other boys from our place and we got steerage passage on a steamer, paying $50 each. Everything was new to me. All my life I had been used to sleeping on a board bed with wooden pillow, and I found the steamer's bunk very uncomfortable, because it was so soft. The food was different from that which I had been used to, and I did not like it at all. I was afraid of the stews, for the thought of what they might be made of by the wicked wizards of the ship made me ill. When I got to San Francisco, which was before the passage of the Exclusion Act, I was half starved, because I was afraid to eat the provisions of the barbarians, but a few days' living in the Chinese quarter made me happy again. A man got me work as a house servant in an American family, and my start was the same as that of almost all the Chinese in this country.

The Chinese laundryman does not learn his trade in China; there are no laundries in China. The women there do the washing in tubs and have no washboards or flat irons. All the Chinese laundrymen here were taught in the first place by American women just as I was taught.

When I went to work for that American family I could not speak a word of English, and I did not know anything about housework. The family consisted of husband, wife, and two children. They were very good to me and paid me $3.50 a week, of which I could save $3.

I did not know how to do anything, and I did not understand what the lady said to me, but she showed me how to cook, wash, iron, sweep, dust, make beds, wash dishes, clean windows, paint and brass, polish the knives and forks, etc., by doing the things herself and then overseeing my efforts to imitate her. She would take my hands and show them how to do things. She and her husband and children laughed at me a great deal, but it was all good natured. I was not confined to the house in the way servants are confined here, but when my work was done in the morning I was allowed to go out till lunchtime. People in California are more generous than they are here.

In six months I had learned how to do the work of our house quite well, and I was getting $5 a week and board, and putting away about $4.25 a week. I had also learned some English, and by going to a Sunday school I learned more English and something about Jesus, who was a great Sage, and whose precepts are like those of Kong-foo-tsze.

It was twenty years ago when I came to this country, and I worked for two years as a servant, getting at the last $35 a month. I sent money home to comfort my parents, but tho I dressed well and lived well and had pleasure, going quite often to the Chinese theater and to dinner parties in Chinatown, I saved $50 in the first six months, $90 in the second, $120 in the third, and $150 in the fourth. So I had $410 at the end of two years, and I was now ready to start in business.

When I first opened a laundry it was in company with a partner, who had been in the business for some years. We went to a town about 500 miles inland, where a railroad was building. We got a board shanty and worked for the men employed by the railroads. Our rent cost was $10 a month and food nearly $5 a week each, for all food was dear and we wanted the best of everything—we lived principally on rice, chickens, ducks, and pork, and did our own cooking. The Chinese take naturally to cooking. It cost us about $50 for our furniture and apparatus, and we made close upon $60 a week, which divided between us. We had to put up with many insults and some frauds, as men would come in and claim parcels that did not belong to them, saying they had lost their tickets, and would fight if they did not get what they asked for. Sometimes we were taken before magistrates and fined for losing shirts that we had never seen. On the other hand, we were making money, and even after sending home $3 a week I was able to save about $15. When the railroad construction gang moved on we went with them. The men were rough and prejudiced against us, but not more so than in the big eastern cities. It is only lately in New York that the Chinese have been able to discontinue putting wire screens in front of their windows, and at the present time the streetboys are still breaking the windows of Chinese laundries all over the city, while the police seem to think it a joke.

We were three years with the railroad, and then went to the mines, where we made plenty of money in gold dust, but had a hard time, for many of the miners were wild men who carried revolvers and after drinking would come into our place to shoot and steal shirts, for which we had to pay. One of these men hit his head hard against a flat iron and all the miners came and broke up our laundry, chasing us out of town. They were going to hang us. We lost all our property and $365 in money, which members of the mob must have found.

Luckily most of our money was in the hands of Chinese bankers in San Francisco. I drew $500 and went east to

Chicago, where I had a laundry for three years, during which I increased my capital to $2,500. After that I was four year in Detroit. I went home to China in 1897, but returned in 1898 and began a laundry business in Buffalo. But Chinese laundry business now is not as good as it was ten years ago. American cheap labor in the steam laundries has hurt it. So I determined to become a general merchant, and with this idea I came to New York and opened a shop in the Chinese quarter, keeping silks, teas, porcelain, clothes, shoes, hats, and Chinese provisions, which include shark's fins and nuts, lily bulbs and lily flowers, lychee nuts, and other Chinese dainties, but do not include rats, because it would be too expensive to import them. The rat which is eaten by the Chinese is a field animal which lives on rice, grain, and sugar cane. Its flesh is delicious. Many Americans who have tasted shark's fin and bird's nest soup and tiger lily flowers and bulbs are firm friends of Chinese cookery. If they could enjoy one of our fine rats they would go to China to live, so as to get some more.

American people eat groundhogs, which are very like these Chinese rats, and they also eat many sorts of food that our people would not touch. Those that have dined with us know that we understand how to live well.

The ordinary laundry shop is generally divided into three rooms. In front is the room where the customers are received, behind that a bedroom and in the back the workshop, which is also the dining room and kitchen. The stove and cooking utensils are the same as those of the Americans.

Work in a laundry begins early on Monday morning— about seven o'clock. There are generally two men, one of whom washes while the other does the ironing. The man who irons does not start in till Tuesday, as the clothes are not ready for him to begin till that time. So he has Sundays and Mondays as holidays. The man who does the washing finishes up on Friday night, and so he has Saturday and Sunday. Each works only five days a week, but those are long days—from seven o'clock in the morning till midnight.

During his holidays the Chinaman gets a good deal of fun out of life. There's a good deal of gambling and some opium smoking, but not so much as Americans imagine. Only a few of New York's Chinamen smoke opium. The habit is very general among rich men and officials in China, but not so much among poor men. I don't think it does as much harm as the liquor that the Americans drink. There's nothing so bad as a drunken man. Opium doesn't make people crazy.

Gambling is mostly fan-tan, but there is a good deal of poker, which the Chinese have learned from Americans and can play very well. They also gamble with dominoes and dice.

The fights among the Chinese and the operations of the hatchet men are all due to gambling. Newspapers often say that they are feuds between the six companies, but that is a mistake. The six companies are purely benevolent societies, which look after the Chinaman when he first lands here. They represent the six southern provinces of China, where most of our people are from, and they are like the German, Swedish, English, Irish, and Italian societies which assist emigrants. When the Chinese keep clear of gambling and opium they are not blackmailed, and they have no trouble with hatchet men or any others.

About *500* of New York's Chinese are Christians, the

others are Buddhists, Taoists, etc., all mixed up. These haven't any Sunday of their own, but keep New York's Day and the first and fifteenth days of each month, when they go to the temple in Mott Street.

In all New York there are only thirty-four Chinese women, and it is impossible to get a Chinese woman out here unless one goes to China and marries her there, and then he must collect affidavits to prove that she really is his wife. That is in the case of a merchant. A laundryman can't bring his wife here under any circumstances, and even the women of the Chinese Ambassador's family had trouble getting in lately.

Is it any wonder, therefore, or any proof of the demoralization of our people if some of the white women in Chinatown are not of good character? What other set of men so isolated and so surrounded by alien and prejudiced people are more moral? Men, wherever they may be, need the society of women, and among the white women of Chinatown are many excellent and faithful wives and mothers.

Recently there has been organized among us the Oriental Club, composed of our most intelligent and influential men. We hope for a great improvement in social conditions by its means, as it will discuss matters that concern us, bring us in closer touch with Americans, and speak for us in something like an official manner.

Some fault is found with us for sticking to our old customs here, especially in the matter of clothes, but the reason is that we find American clothes much inferior, so far as comfort and warmth go, The Chinaman's coat for the winter is very durable, very light, and very warm. It is easy and not in the way. If he wants to work he slips out of it in a moment and can put it on again as quickly. Our shoes and hats also are better, we think, for our purposes, than the American clothes. Most of us have tried the American clothes, and they make us feel as if we were in the stocks.

I have found out, during my residence in this country, that much of the Chinese prejudice against Americans is unfounded, and I no longer put faith in the wild tales that were told about them in our village, tho some of the Chinese, who have been here twenty years and who are learned men, still believe that there is no marriage in this country, that the land is infested with demons, and that all the people are given over to general wickedness.

I know better. Americans are not all bad, nor are they wicked wizards. Still, they have their faults, and their treatment of us is outrageous.

The reason why so many Chinese go into the laundry business in this country is because it requires little capital and is one of the few opportunities that are open. Men of other nationalities who are jealous of the Chinese, because he is a more faithful worker than one of their people, have raised such a great outcry about Chinese cheap labor that they have shut him out of working on farms or in factories or building railroads or making streets or digging sewers. He cannot practice any trade, and his opportunities to do business are limited to his own countrymen. So he opens a laundry when he quits domestic service.

The treatment of the Chinese in this country is all wrong and mean. It is persisted in merely because China is not a fighting nation. The Americans would not dare to treat Germans, English, Italians, or even Japanese as they treat the Chinese, because if they did there would be a war.

There is no reason for the prejudice against the Chinese.

The cheap labor cry was always a falsehood. Their labor was never cheap, and is not cheap now. It has always commanded the highest market price. But the trouble is that the Chinese are such excellent and faithful workers that bosses will have no others when they can get them. If you look at men working on the street you will find an overseer for every four or five of them. That watching is not necessary for Chinese. They work as well when left to themselves as they do when someone is looking at them.

It was the jealousy of laboring men of other nationalities—especially the Irish—that raised all the outcry against the Chinese. No one would hire an Irishman, German, Englishman, or Italian when he could get a Chinese, because our countrymen are so much more honest, industrious, steady, sober, and painstaking. Chinese were persecuted, not for their vices, but for their virtues. There never was any honesty in the pretended fear of leprosy or in the cheap labor scare, and the persecution continues still, because Americans make a mere practice of loving justice. They are all for money-making, and they want to be on the strongest side always. They treat you as a friend while you are prosperous, but if you have a misfortune they don't know you. There is nothing substantial in their friendship.

Wu-Ting-Fang talked very plainly to Americans about their ill treatment of our countrymen, but we don't see any good results. We hoped for good from Roosevelt, we thought him a brave and good man, but yet he has continued the exclusion of our countrymen, though all other nations are allowed to pour in here—Irish, Italians, Jews, Poles, Greeks, Hungarians, etc. It would not have been so if Mr. McKinley had lived.

Irish fill the almshouses and prisons and orphan asylums; Italians are among the most dangerous of men; Jews are unclean and ignorant. Yet they are all let in, while Chinese, who are sober, or duly law abiding, clean, educated, and industrious, are shut out. There are few Chinamen in jails and none in the poor houses. There are no Chinese tramps or drunkards. Many Chinese here have become sincere Christians, in spite of the persecution which they have to endure from their heathen countrymen. More than half the Chinese in this country would become citizens if allowed to do so, and would be patriotic Americans. But how can they make this country their home as matters now are! They are not allowed to bring wives here from China, and if they marry American women there is a great outcry.

All Congressmen acknowledge the injustice of the treatment of my people, yet they continue it. They have no backbone.

Under the circumstances, how can I call this my home, and how can any one blame me if I take my money and go back to my village in China?

A Japanese Immigrant:
Becoming a Servant

After Chinese immigration to the United States was halted by the U.S. Congress in 1882 at the urging of the American Federation of Labor, the country's need for menial labor stimulated Japanese immigration. From 1901 to 1910, some 130,000 Japanese arrived, and most settled in California.

White Americans seemed to transfer their fear of Chinese to these newcomers from Asia after 1901, when California governor Henry Gage called the Japanese as much of a "peril" as the Chinese. The San Francisco Chronicle *next entitled a frightening front-page series of articles "The Japanese Invasion, The Problem of the Hour."*

A Japanese Immigrant

White citizens also had hit upon a unique reason to detest these newcomers—Japanese were often willing to adopt American customs. They became the first group to endure suspicion and hatred because of their ability to "be American."

The immigrant author of the following autobiography asked that his name be withheld because of his frank criticism for his new homeland and some wealthy people he worked for. An ardent student, he sprinkled his narrative with literary references gleaned from his reading in American fiction.

My destination was Portland, Oregon, where my cousin is studying. Before I took a boat in Puget Sound to Tacoma, Washington, we have to be examined by the immigration officer. To my surprise these officers looked to me like a plain citizen—no extravagant dignity, no authoritative air. I felt so envious, I said to myself, "Ah! Indeed this is the characteristic of democracy, equality of personal right so well shown." I respect the officers more on this account. They asked me several questions. I answered with my broken English I have learned at Yokohama Commercial School. Finally they said: "So you are a student? How much money have you at hand?" I showed them $50. The law requires $30. The officers gave me a piece of stamped paper—certificate—to permit me go into the United States. I left Victoria 8 p.m. and arrived Tacoma, Washington, 6 a.m. Again I have surprised with the muddy streets and the dirty wharf. I thought the wharf of Yokohama is hundred times better. Next morning I left for Portland, Oregon.

Great disappointment and regret I have experienced when I was told that I, the boy of 17 years old, smaller in stature indeed than ordinary 14 years old American boy, imperfect in English knowledge, I can be any use here, but become a domestic servant, as the field for Japanese very narrow and limited. Thus reluctantly I have submitted to be a recruit of the army of domestic servants of which I ever dreamed up to this time. The place where I got to work in the first time was a boarding house. My duties were to peel potatoes, wash the dishes, a few laundry work, and also I was expected to do whatever mistress, waitress and cook has told me.

When I first entered the kitchen wearing a white apron what an uncomfortable and mortifying feeling I experienced. I thought I shall never be able to proceed the work. I felt as if I am pressed down on my shoulder with loaded tons of weight. My heart palpitates. I did not know what I am and what to say. I stood by the door of kitchen motionless like a stone, with a dumbfound silence. The cook gave me a scornful look and said nothing. Perhaps at her first glance she perceived me entirely unfit to be her help. A kindly looking waitress, slender, alert Swedish girl, sympathetically put the question to me if I am first time to work. Said she, "Oh! Well, you will get learn and soon be used to it!" as if she has fully understand the situation. Indeed, this ordinary remarks were such a encouragement. She and cook soon opened the conference how to rescue me. In a moment I was to the mercy of Diana of the kitchen like Arethusa. Whistling up the courage I started to work. The work being entirely new and also such as unaccustomed one, I felt exceedingly unpleasant and hard. Sonorous voice from the cook of my slowness in peeling potatoes often vibrated into my tympanum. The waitress occasionally called out for the butter plates and saucers at the top of her displeasing voice. Frequently the words "Hurry up!" were added. I always noticed her lips at the motion rather than hands. The proprietor, an old lady, painstakingly taught me to work how. Almost always commencing the phrase "I show you" and ending "Did you understand?" The words were so prominently sounded; finally made me tired of it and latter grew hated to hear of it. Taking the advantage of my green hand Diana of kitchen often unloaded hers to me. Thus I have been working almost all the time from 5:30 a.m. to 9 p.m. When I got through the day's work I was tired.

Things went on, however, fairly well for the first six days, forgetting my state and trying to adapt my own into the environment. But when Sunday come all my subsided emotions sprung up, recollecting how pleasantly I used spend the holidays. This memory of past pleasure vast contrast of the present one made me feel ache. What would the boys in Japan say if they found me out. I am thus employed in the kitchen receiving the orders from the maidservant whom I have once looked down and thought never to be equal while I was dining at my uncle's house. I feel the home-sick. I was so lonesome and so sorry that I came to America. Ignoring the kind advice of my friends, rejecting the offer of help from my uncle at home, quickened by my youthful sentiment to be the independent, and believing the work alone to be noble, I came to this county to educate myself worthy to my father's name. How beautiful idea it was while it existed in imagination, but how hard it is

when it came to practice. There was no honor, no responsibility, no sense of duty, but the pliancy of servitude was
the cardinal requirement. There is no personal liberty while
your manhood is completely ignored.

Subduing my vanity, overcoming from the humiliation
and swallowing down all the complaints, weariness and
discouragement, I went on one week until Sunday. In spite
of my determination to face into the world, manly defending
my own in what I have within, together with my energy
and ability, I could not resist the offspring from my bro-
ken-hearted emotions. Carrying the heavy and sad heart
I was simply dragged by the day's routine work. The old
lady inquired me if I am not sick. I replied, "No." Thank
enough for a first time she gave me a chance to rest from 1
o'clock to 4 afternoon. Sooner I retired into my room,
locked the door, throwing the apron away. I cast myself
down on the bed and sobbed to my heart contention. Thus
let out all my suppressed emotion of grief from the morning. You might laugh at me, yet none the less it was a true
state of my mind at that moment. After this free outburst
of my passion I felt better. I was keenly felt the environment was altogether not congenial. I noticed myself I am
inclining considerably sensitive.

After I stay there about ten days I asked the old lady
that I should be discharged. She wanted me to state the
reason. My real objection was that the work was indeed
too hard and unpleasant for me to bear and also there were
not time even to read a book. But I thought it is rather
impolite to say so and partly my strange pride hated to
confess my weakness, fearing the reflection as a lazy boy.
Really I could not think how smoothly I should tell my
reasons. So I kept silent rather with a stupefied look. She

suggested me if the work were not too hard. It was just the point, but how foolish I was; I did positively denied. "Then why can you not stay here?" she went on. I said, childishly, "I have nothing to complain; simply I wants to go back to New York. My passion wants to." Then she smiled and said, "Poor boy; you better think over; I shall I speak to you tomorrow." Next day she told me how she shall be sorry to lose me just when I have began to be handy to her after the hard task to taught me work how. Tactfully she persuaded me to stay. At the end of second week I asked my wages, but she refused on the ground that if she does I might leave her. Day by day my sorrow and regret grew stronger. My heavy heart made me feel so hard to work. At that moment I felt as if I am in the prison assigned to the hard labor. My coveted desire was to be freed from the yoke of this old lady. Believing the impossibility to obtain her sanction, early in the next morning while everybody still in the bed, I hide my satchel under the bush in the back yard. When mistress went on market afternoon, while everybody is busy, I have jumped out from the window and climbed up the fence to next door and slip away. Leaving the note and wages behind me, I hurried back to Japanese Christian Home.

Since then I have tried a few other places with a better success at each trial and in course of time I have quite accustomed to it and gradually become indifferent as the humiliation melted down.

Next position I had was in New York—a family of up-to-date fashionable mistress. I was engaged as a butler. I have surprised the formality she observe. The way to open the door, salute the guest, language to be used according to the rank of the guests and how to handle the name card.

Characteristic simplicity of democracy could not be seen in this household. I am distinctly felt I am a servant, as the mistress artificially created the wide gap between her and me. Her tone of speech were imperial dignity. I have only to obey her mechanically and perform automatically the assigned duty. To me this state of things were exceedingly dull. I know I am servant full well, yet I wished to be treated as a man. I thought she is so accustomed the sycophancy and servility of the servants she could not help but despise them. Perhaps the experience forced her to think the servants cannot be trusted and depended upon. I thought I might be able to improve the situation by convincing her my efficiency and also I have no mercenary spirit. Tho the position may be disgraceful one, I consoled my own, hoping to make it pure and exalt little higher by the recognition of my personality by my master and mistress. I was anxious to find out of my mistress's strongest principle of her self-regard. I have carefully listened her conversation in the dining table with her husband, of whom I regretfully observed the traces of the hard-hearted and close-fisted selfishness, and at the afternoon tea with her friends. But each occasion made me feel disappointed. One day she told me go out get for her the cigarettes. Out of my surprise I said to her, "Do you smoke?" I had not a least bit of idea that the respectful American lady would smoke. I was plainly told that I am her servant. I got to obey whatever she wants to. Same afternoon I have been told to serve the afternoon tea. The mistress seeing the tea cup, said to me, "No, no; put the glass for the champagne, of course." I was once more surprise. Meantime the luxuriously dressed, pretty looking creatures whom, when I met at the hallway, they were so dignified with the majestic air and impressed me as if they were the living angels; but, to my utter disgust, these fair, supposed innocent sex drunk and smoke like men do. Next day I tendered my resignation to my ladyship.

Altho I has been advocated the gospel of wealth and extolled the rich, I hate the rich people who display their wealth and give me a tip in a boastful manner. I felt I am insulted and I have protested. Sometime the tip was handed down indirectly from the hands of the captain. Each time when I have obliged to take the tip I am distinctly felt "the gift without giver is bare." I, however, thankfully accepted the offer from a lady who give me the money in such a kind and sympathetic manner. A gentleman gave one dollar, saying, "I wish this were ten times as much; still I want you keep it for me to help your study." Indeed this one dollar how precious I felt. Once a fastidious lady was on the board. She used to kick one thing to another. Of course I did not pay any attention. Whenever she scold me, I said at heart, "It's your pleasure to blame me, lady. I, on my part, simply to hear you. I am not almighty; I cannot be a perfect. If I made mistake I shall correct. You might bully me as you please and treat me like a dog, I shall not object. I have a soul within me. My vital energy in self-denying struggle could not be impaired by your despise. On the contrary, it will be stimulated." That the way I used swallowed down all the reprimand she gave me. I, however, getting tired to hear her sharp tongue and hoping to be on the good term with her. One morning I have exerted an exceptionally good care to clean her cabin. Right after I got through her compartment she called me back and told me that I did not take a good care of. I replied emphatically with a conviction, "I did my best under the circumstance." But she insisted I must do better next time. Then she took out a dollar bill, gave it to me. I refused to take it. She thrust the money into my hand. I have thrown back the paper money to her feet. "Madam, this is the bribe and graft. I am amply paid from the owner of the yacht to serve you," said I. "No, madam; no tip for me." Without waiting her answer, while she seemed taken entirely surprised, I quickly withdrew from her. Since then she has entirely changed her attitude toward me.

While I was working on the boat I noticed the cook making a soup from a spring chicken and a good size of fine roast beef. I am amazed of the extravagant use of the material. I asked him why he do not use the soup meat and a cheaper roaster for making the soup. I was told it's none of my business and get out from the place. Daily I witnessed the terrible scene of wasting the food. I often thought something ought to be done. It's just economic crime. The foodstuff cook thrown away overboard would be more than enough to support five families in the East Side. Yet the fellow honored as an excellent cook and especially praised of his soup!

The owner of the yacht and mistress were very agreeable persons; the children, too, were also lovely and good-natured youngsters. I shall never forget the kindness and consideration shown by them. While I am waiting on the table I have often drawn into the conversation. The mistress, unlike the wife who commands an enormous fortune, possessed a good common sense and has a sensible judgment in treating of her dependence, as she was cultured lady. The owner of the boat was the man of affairs; a broadminded man he was. He has had struggling days in his early life. He has shown me great deal of sympathy. I did indeed "just love" to serve them, as one of the sailors has said to me.

Next summer I have been told by Mr. C. to work his yacht again. He said he would pay me $40 per month and if I stayed whole season he would add to it $100. "This $100 is not charity; it my appreciation for your self-denying struggle, to help your school expenses," said he. How hard it was to reject for such a kind offer. I asked two days for the answer. Finally I have decided to refuse, as I had some reasons to believe there are possibility to develop my ability in another direction more congenial line. For days I did not hear from him. I thought I am sure he has angered me. I was waiting the occasion to explain to him fully and apologize. About a month later I got the message to come to his office. To my surprise Mr. C. told me he would give me $50 at the fall to help me out my school expenses. He said, "I am interested with you. You will be a great man some day. I wanted to express by appreciation to the 'hard spot within you.'" IIow gratefully I felt. I did not find the suitable phrase to express my thanks, so I simply said, "Thank you." But inwardly I did almost worshiped him. I felt I am not alone in this world. What encouragement Mr. C.'s words to me; I felt as tho I got the reinforcement of one regiment.

Shall I stop here with this happy memory? Yet before I close this confession I cannot pass on without disclosing a few incidence I suffered from the hands of inconsiderate millionaire. About three years ago I have worked as a butler in a millionaire's mansion at N.J. Mistress was the young lady about twenty-three years old and the master was forty-five years old. Every morning mistress would not get up till eleven o'clock. Master gets up six. So we servants serve twice breakfast. At the dinner often mistress and master served the different sort of food. One day I was sick and asked three days absent to consult Japanese physician in New York. According the advice of doctor I have written twice asking to be given two more days to rest. I did not get answer. After I stay out five days I took 1:30 p.m. train from Jersey City; returned house 4 p.m. As soon as I entered the mansion the master told me I am discharged. This was the reward for my faithful service of eight months. I wanted to know the reason for. He simply said he wants to have waitress and told me to hurry to pack up my belonging and leave instantly. I asked, however, the reference to be given. He said he would send forward to New York by mail. I was everything ready in one hour; left his mansion at 5 p.m. to the station, where I waited one hour and a half. I returned New York again 9 p.m., with hunger and exhausted from emotion, as I am not quite recovered from my illness. Since then three times I asked the reference; he never answered. Until now it is quite mystery what made him angry me. His action handicapped me greatly to hunt new place.

Greatest trouble and disadvantage to be a domestic servant is that he has to be absolutely subjected under the emotional rule of the mistress. No amount of candid or rational argument will avail. No matter how worthy your dissenting opinion be, if it does not please your mistress you have to suffer for it. Once I worked for a widow lady whose incomes are derived from the real estate, stock and bonds. She is economizing so strictly that often handicapped me. One day, taking the chances of her good humor, I told her that her well meant efforts are the misapplication of her energy, trying to save her pin money through the economy of gas bill and grocery bill in the old-fashioned way, while neglecting to avail herself to the "modern high finance scheme" hereby she may improve her resources. The reward of this speech was an honorable discharge! To be a successful servant is to make yourself a fool. This habitual submission will bring a lamentable effect to the one's brain function. Day after day throughout the years confined into the kitchen and dining-room, physically tired, unable to refresh yourself in the way of mental reciprocity, even the bright head will suffer if stay too long as a servant. Of course, one's character will be greatly improved and refined by serving the employer like Mr. C. and Mrs. B. But they are exception. Majority of employer will not be interested in their servants.

The motive of my engaging in the domestic work, no matter how meritorious it may intrinsically be, our people look with me the scornful eyes if not with positive despise. The doors of prominent Japanese family closed before me. Sometimes I was unrecognized by the fellow students from Japan, who are sons of wealth. I wrote one day a few lines to console myself:

Who does scorn the honest toil
Mayest ungraceful post thou hail
When the motive is true and pure
The wealth of learning to store.

O! never say that my humble lot
Does harm the fame of fortunate sons
Of Yamato. Disgrace me not.
How wilt thou feel, were it thine once.

THE CRUEL YEARS

How I suffer within knowest thou not;
Aspiring hope alone animates weary heart.
Year after year and day after day
Over the rough sea I steer my destiny

Unknown to shape my destination
My heart sobered with resignation.
But far from to be the misanthropist
The love of life giving the keener zest.

I kneel down for the silent prayer
Concealing my own I toil and prepare
To realize the hope dear to my heart
And absorbed the whole my thought.

O what joy how blessed I am!
With inspiring hope for my future aim
To consecrate my own for Truth and Humanity,
To this end I devote with honor and sincerity.

Some says Japanese are studying while they are working in the kitchen, but it is all nonsense. Many of them started so, but nearly all of them failed. It is all well up to college, where there are not much references need to read. After you have served dinner, washing dishes and cleaning dining-room, you are often tired when you commence to write an essay. You will feel sometime your fingers are stiff and your arms are ache. In the afternoon, just when you began concentrated on the points in the book, the front door bell rung—the goods delivered from the stores, or callers to mistress, or telephone messages and what not. How often you are disturbed while you have to read at least three hours succession quietly in order to make the outline and dug up all the essential points. I have experience, once I attended lecture after I have done a rush work in the kitchen. I was so tired felt as tho all the blood in the body rushing up to the brain and partly sleepy. My hands would not work. I could not take the note of professor's lecture, as my head so dull could not order to my hand what professor's lecture was.

Many Japanese servants has told me as soon as they saved sufficient amount of money they would start the business. But many young Japanese, while their intentions are laudable, they will find the vile condition of environment in a large city like New York has a greater force than their moral courage could resist. Disheartened from the hard work or excessive disagreeableness of their environment often tempt them to seek a vain comfort in the misdirected quarter; thus dissipate their preciously earned money. Even those who have saved money successfully for the capital to start the business, their future is quite doubtful. When they have saved enough money it will be a time that their business ability melted away or by no means are sharp. Years' husbanding of domestic work, handicapped and over-interfered by mistress, their mental agilities are reduced to the lamentable degree. Yet, matured by these undesirable experience, most of them are quite unconscious of this outcome as little by little submissive and depending habit so securely rooted within their mind. It will be an exceedingly hard to adjust themselves immediately to the careful and shrewd watch required in the modern business enterprise, tho they may be assisted by the instinct of self-interest. Most deliberate reflection is required from these unconscious servile habit of action to restore to their previous independent thinking mind. The sooner they quit the kitchen the better, tho needless to say there are a few exceptions.

Above all I am so grateful to the members of the Japanese Consulate, prominent citizens of our colony, editors of Japanese papers, ministers and secretaries of Japanese missions co-operating each other to help out young Japanese to secure their more agreeable and harmless position, and also they are throwing their good influence to induce Japanese domestic servants to go over to Korea and Manchuria to become a pioneer and land owner in these country, instead of to be the co-worker with the Venus in the American commissary department.

Elizabeth G. Flynn: Becoming a High School Rebel

Born in 1890 to an Irish immigrant family with a tradition of religious and political dissent, Elizabeth Gurley Flynn grew up in the South Bronx and attended Morris High School. She developed a passion for working-class politics, a striking talent for public speaking, and an independent spirit.

Political and economic inequality at the turn of the century drove an untold number of ordinary people to devote their lives to social activism. Though she never held public office, tried to make money, or gain a high station in life, Flynn was one of those who found fulfillment fighting for justice, free speech, and a society based on cooperation rather than competition.

Since her revolutionary approach appalled more people than it persuaded, historians have chosen to ignore her, and others have dismissed her as misguided, deluded, or a pariah. Her autobiography, Rebel Girl, *with its informal but powerful writing style, displays her committment to working people and her outrage at privilege based on money, race, gender, or class.*

There were tight social lines drawn between the "lace curtain" Irish of my mother's family and the "shanty Irish" of my father's family. The difficulties he had in courting my mother are indicated by the fact that neither Gurleys nor Flynns came to their wedding. My father was determined to leave the quarry. All but one of his male relatives had died as a result of working there. My father carried the mark of the quarry to his grave. When he was a young boy, working in a quarry in Maine carrying tools, the sight of one eye was destroyed by a flying chip of granite. He lived to be over 80 "thanks to Mama," we always said, who encouraged him in his ambition. . . .

We finally arrived in New York City at the turn of the century, in 1900. My mother was tired of moving around and decided here we would stay. Our school terms had been interrupted and what little furniture we possessed was being smashed up in moving around. We came to Aunt Mary, a widow and a tailoress, who lived with her five children in the South Bronx. Soon they found a flat for us nearby. It was on the inside facing an airshaft, gaslit, with cold water. The only heat was the kitchen stove. We three older children cried, we refused to unpack our toys . . . .

We were horrified, too, at the conditions we had never met in our travels elsewhere — the prevalence of pests in the old slum houses, mice, rats, cockroaches and bedbugs. My poor mother carried on a desperate struggle to rid us of these parasites. . . .

On cold winter days we'd huddle in the kitchen and shut off the rest of the house. We would do our lessons by a kerosene lamp when the gas was shut off for nonpayment. We'd undress in the kitchen, scurry to the cold bedrooms, all the children sleeping in one bed, where we put our coats over us to keep warm. We might as well have lived on an isolated farm in the Dakotas for all the good the benefits of the great city did us then. Bill collectors harassed my gentle mother—the landlord, the gas man, the milk man, the grocer. Once she bought us an encyclopedia on the installment plan. But she couldn't keep up the payments and our hearts were broken when we lost the beautiful books we treasured so highly. . . .

I attended the grammar school, P.S. No. 9 on 138th Street. It was a decrepit old building then, with toilets in the yard. . . . My teacher in an upper grade was James A. Hamilton who was studying law and later became a New York State official. He fired me with ambition to be a constitutional lawyer and drilled us so thoroughly in the U.S. Constitution and especially the Bill of Rights that I have been defending it ever since. (I have been arrested at least ten times in my lifetime and in every instance the denial of the Bill of Rights has been involved.) I joined a debating society which Mr. Hamilton had organized and took to it like a duck to water. I won a gold medal for proficiency in debating and one in English at graduation in 1904. . . . I remember arguing that women should vote—and strongly believing what I advocated. . . .

Someone at the Harlem Socialist Club, hearing of my debating experience and knowing of my reading and intense interest in socialism, asked me to make a speech. My father was not much impressed with the idea. He thought they should have asked him to expound Marxism, on which he now considered himself an expert. I'm afraid my father would be labelled a "male-supremacist" these days. Once I stood up at a meeting and asked the speaker a question. He frowned upon such a performance. Couldn't I have asked him to explain on our way home? But my mother encouraged me and I accepted the offer to speak. I tried to select a subject upon which my father would not interfere too much, something he did not consider too important. It was "What Socialism Will Do For Women."

Wednesday, January 31, 1906, is a date engraved on my memory, the occasion of my first public speech. . . . I was a slender serious girl, not yet 16, with my black hair loose to my waist, tied with a ribbon. I wore a long full skirt down to my ankles, as was proper in 1906, a white shirt waist and a red tie. I had labored to write my speech and had stubbornly resisted all attempts of . . . my father and others to tell me what to say or to actually write it for me. Good or bad, I felt it had to be my own. I began to quake inwardly at the start, facing an adult audience for the first time. But they were sympathetic and I was soon sailing along serenely. When I concluded, I asked for questions, as I had heard other speakers do. None were forthcoming. The audience apparently sensed that I was nervous. How they laughed when I said resentfully: "Just because I'm young and a girl, is no reason you shouldn't ask me questions!"

My advent as a speaker caused no comment outside of the weekly Socialist paper, *The Worker,* which said: "In view of her youth, although knowing she was very bright, the comrades were prepared to judge her lecture indulgently; they found that no indulgence was called for that she had a surprising grasp of the subject and handled it with skill." With this blessing I was launched on my career as a public speaker. . . .

In August 1906, I was arrested with my father and several others for "speaking without a permit" and "blocking traffic" at 38th Street and Broadway, then the heart of the theatrical district. . . .When the police officer ordered us to stop, we refused and the reserves were called. Our arrests followed.

We were released on bail at 2 a.m. and appeared before Magistrate Walsh in Jefferson Market Court the next day. . . . We were all discharged, with the judge advising me to go back to school that Fall and be a student a while longer before I become a teacher. . . . *The New York Times* editorialized in a humorous, patronizing style about "the ferocious Socialist haranguer, Miss Flynn, who will graduate at school in two years and whose shoe tops at present show below her skirts, [who] tells us what to think, which is just what she thinks." Pop never forgave Mr. Pentecost. "That damned lawyer wouldn't let me talk!" he'd rave.

Strangely enough, when I returned to Morris High School in the Fall, no comment was made on the arrest. But attending school by day and meetings by night was a heavy toll, not conducive to proper rest or study. I had an excellent scholastic record in grammar school with all A marks, but it had now declined alarmingly. Mr. Denbigh, the principal, tried to convince me that I should concentrate on my studies and give up the outside activities, of which he expressed no criticism. He said if I finished my education I would be better equipped for work in the labor movement a few years later. My mother agreed with Mr. Denbigh. But I was impatient. It did not seem to me that anything I was learning there had a relationship to life or would be helpful to me. With the Revolution on my mind I found it difficult to concentrate on Latin or geometry. And I smarted under the "too young" attitude of adults. So within the next few months I left school, an action I deeply regretted in later years. . . .

My first personal strike experience was in Bridgeport, Connecticut in the summer of 1907 with the Tube Mill workers, largely Hungarian. . . . Here, for the first time, I participated in strike committee meetings, mass picketing and daily meetings in two languages, with sad Hungarian violin music for entertainment. . . . The strike meetings were in the vicinity of the mill, where the workers lived. In the evening we went downtown and held street meetings on a main thoroughfare to acquaint the people of the city with the conditions and the demands of the striking workers. We gained considerable support this way, which helped to settle the strike. . . .

. . . My first participation in an IWW free speech fight and my second arrest occurred in [Missoula, Montana], not an industrial town but a gateway to many lumber camps and mining areas. . . .

We held street meetings on one of the principal corners and drew large crowds, mainly the migratory workers who flocked in and out of town. We had rented as an IWW hall a large roomy space in the basement of the leading theater and were rapidly recruiting members into the organization. The storekeepers objected to our meetings, especially the employment agencies, which we attacked mercilessly. Under their pressure the City Council passed an ordinance as unconstitutional, a violation of the First Amendment guaranteeing freedom of speech. . . . When we tried to hold meetings, two were arrested the first night and dismissed with a warning not to speak again. Four were arrested the second night. . . . Our Missoula free speechers were sentenced to 15 days in the county jail. Those of us who were left planned the mass tactics which were advocated in free speech fights, of which Missoula was one of the first examples.

We sent out a call to all "foot-loose rebels to come at once—to defend the Bill of Rights." A steady stream of IWW members began to flock in, by freight cars—on top, inside and below. As soon as one speaker was arrested, another took his place. The jail was soon filled and the cell under the firehouse was turned into an additional jail. The excrement from the horses leaked through and made this place so unbearable that the IWW prisoners protested by song and speech, night and day. They were directly across the street from the city's main hotel and the guests complained of the uproar. The court was nearby and its proceedings were disrupted by the noise. People came to listen to the hubbub, until finally all IWWs were taken back to the county jail.

The fire department turned the hose on one of the meetings, but the townspeople protested vigorously against this after several people were hurt. College professors at the university took up the cudgels for free speech, especially when another woman, Mrs. Edith Frenette, and I were arrested. We were treated with kid gloves by the sheriff and his wife. . . .

Eventually, the townspeople got tired of the unfavorable publicity and excitement. The taxpayers were complaining of the cost to the little city, demanding it be reduced. . . . Finally, the authorities gave up. All cases were dropped, and we were allowed to resume our meetings. We returned to our peaceful pursuit of agitating and organizing the IWW. I liked Missoula and hated to leave. . . .

. . . . I could never hear enough of the life and adventures of the lumberjacks and miners who dropped in regularly. But Spokane called me to their free speech fight. "When loud and clear the call I hear, I must arise and go!" I went in December 1909, although I was again pregnant.

Anna Louise: Entering White Womanhood

*Born in Friend, Nebraska, in 1885 to a Congregational min-
ister father and a college-educated mother, Anna Louise Strong
raced toward a dissenting womanhood. As she scaled society's
tallest walls, she relished the challenge and adventure and
scoffed at fierce disapproval.*

*Unlike many other young women, Anna Louise succeeded
admirably. At twenty-three she became the youngest woman
to earn a doctorate degree in philosophy at the University of
Chicago. She became a world traveler and noted author, only
to be deemed a pariah by many because of her enthusiastic
support of communism in the Soviet Union and China. By*

1968, when she died single and unrepentant in China, few would deny that she had lived her life as she wished.

Charging uphill began early for young Anna Louise, as she revealed in her autobiography, written in 1935.

My first contacts with the world outside my home had shown me that by no means everybody loved me. My parents had told me to be good and love everybody, and then everybody would love me. But they didn't; certainly not everybody. Sometimes it was the older girls who plainly didn't want me about; sometimes it was boys. A painful feeling began to grow of being generally not wanted. I felt in terms of great generalities. I wanted everybody to like me; I felt that nobody did. My standards were too demanding; if they were less kind than my mother, I thought they didn't like me at all, and that something was the matter with me. . . .

From this haunting feeling of being not wanted, which remained a recurrent haunt through life, I found two ways of escape, both of which in changing form also persisted. One was the invention of gods, the other was personal efficiency in work. My early heaven was commanded to furnish companionship—and did. It offered raptures of thought transference. Words were so difficult; they never gave my exact meaning. How wonderful if one could think and have the exactness of the thought repeated to a loved person far across the world! . . .

When high school courses demanded specialization in study, I abandoned soul-mates in favor of "living a thousand lives." It was stupid to be just one person; one person could never do all the interesting things there are to do. I wanted to be a North Pole explorer, and an airman, and a great writer, and a mother of ten—one child wasn't worth the time! There were at least ten lives that I simply had to live, and I knew if I started to think, I could make it a thousand. Yet all these lives must be linked into one person who could know and enjoy them all. I gave it up; it was too complicated. . . .

I lived in a comfortable family in a comfortable suburb—it was now Oak Park, near Chicago—where nobody was very poor. There were thousands of these residential suburbs in American life. In them lived not only the well-to-do, but also people of moderate means, among whom we were classed. "Workers" also lived there, skilled building workers, railwaymen, other skilled trades. No one in these suburbs ever spoke of distinctions of class, but only of good society, into which all were pushing. We didn't see men of the steel towns or textile mills. . . .

I was still in my early teens when I discovered the poverty of Chicago's west side; I went there to teach sewing in settlement classes. I was told that this poverty was due to ignorance; these people were not yet developed. I never thought of them as a different "class." They were just immigrants from a more backward world who had not yet attained the polished prosperity which America gave. They would go to schools (my sewing classes were such schools) and play in the city playgrounds which Chicago so magnificently built. Then they, or at least their children, would be American like us. Clean, contented, efficient, prosperous was what "American" meant. America was "God's country," a country without classes, the best and freest country in the world.

As I grew somewhat older, some perplexities invaded our home from the trips my mother made to organize women's societies in the southern parts of Illinois. There she saw mining towns, real Americans in some cases who suffered and went on strike. She gave me no details but I remember her depression when she came home on one occasion and said: "There is much injustice in the world; it is hard to understand it. Some people are very hard and greedy and grab much more than their share; they refuse to hear the rights of others. Many people suffer because of them, yet nobody punishes them. I think now that she must have tried to argue with some mine-owner about the condition of the miners and come face to face with a naked capitalism that bewildered her.

I clearly remember about this time—it was in my middle teens—my mother rushed up to a colored woman and embraced her on the street, telling that this was Molly Church, one of her best-loved classmates from Oberlin College. I showed no great warmth over the introduction; my early love for "the colors" had evaporated under the influence of schoolmates. I had even written a poem for the high school paper, "Remember the Maine"; it was the time of the Spanish War and I was on the high road to becoming a young imperialist. As soon as the woman left, my mother reproved me, saying that if I had any feelings against people on account of the color of their skin, these were bad feelings which I must at once overcome. She added that bad people made it very hard for Negroes to get education and equal rights and that when a Negro succeeded in doing it, as her classmate had, she had shown much more courage than I had every shown or than most white people possessed. She was therefore entitled to special honor. I wished that the classmate might come back that I might show how splendid I now understood her to be. . . .

It was after my mother's death that I first questioned my father's religious theories. He had preached a children's sermon on "cheap girls," meaning girls who gave their caresses too easily to boys, without waiting until they were sure they had discovered the chosen one, who would properly prize them. He had preached it earlier in a different city when I was younger and it had impressed me. But now I was in my late teens and I discovered discrepancies in his views.

"I don't think this talk about cheap girls goes well with Christian ethics," I told him. "Jesus tells us to love everybody and to give all we have to the world without questioning the return, and when people injure us we are to forgive 'till seventy times seven.' But now you say girls are to hold back and not give themselves until they are properly prized. I see very well one mustn't be easy with one's kisses. All the same, it would be really more Christian to be 'easy.' It wouldn't be safe to be quite Christian."

My father was worried. "I am only trying to save you from ruin," he answered.

"That's another difference between us," I persisted. "You think there are just two things that can ruin a girl, either an unhappy marriage or a love affair without marriage. Well, I think either of those would be horrible tragedy but I wouldn't let either of them ruin me permanently. I'd get out of it somehow. I don't think either of them is what the novels call 'worse than death,' for when you are dead, you are finished."

My father shrank from my lightness. Though he had become unusually broad-minded for his generation on the question of divorce and fallen women, for his own family he accepted the view that the first sexual experience of a girl either establishes her or ruins her. He had rejected property marriage with disdain, yet he cherished uncritically the ethics derived from it.

Nor did I myself escape those ethics. In spite of my protest that "nothing a man could do to me could permanently ruin me" I really thought of marriage as the great decisive choice of life which would determine all my future and to which any previous schemes of my own must be sacrificed.

I even chose my future work with reference to its possible subordination in marriage. Writing seemed to me an admirable occupation because it could be done in any part of the world to which my husband might take me, and could even be accomplished in odd moments at home. I tried to avoid having opinions which were too fixed and definite, which might some day have to be changed to fit a married state. I reasoned that I must have some work of my own and save a little money in order to be independent in case I should disagree with my husband, and not be a burden on him in case we happily agreed. If I did all these things then when the master of my fate at last arrived, I should be ready to adapt myself to anything he might demand.

That I really looked on such a future husband as the master of my fate is clear from a conversation I had when I was already twenty with some highly sophisticated members of the faculty of the University of Chicago. By this time I was going about with older men who were attracted and amused by my combination of youthful freshness with noticeable brains. One of them teased me as an "unmastered girl who doesn't want a master."

"Oh, but I do," I cried. "I want to find someone who will tell me just what I must do about everything and then I will do it. I will never have to decide for myself again."

Yes, it was really a god I wanted, a boss, a master, a parent who would continue infancy for me. People told me that it was feminine to want this; and I believed in my soul, a soul already molded by the emotions of religion into the mood of adoring dependence, that they were right. Yet against this mood there warred the contradictory demand for freedom, which I was winning through the personal efficiency taught in the schools. My own life, my own work, my own career already threatened to become interesting and to make me less adaptable, less ready to give them up at the whim of some male. I reconciled these contradictory cravings for a boss and for freedom by telling myself that I would not give myself till I found somebody worth it, somebody sufficiently important and wonderful so that I should not mind putting all my life into one parcel and handing it over to him.

The girls of my day discussed the word "obey" in the stricter forms of church marriage, alternately adoring it and shivering away from it. Although the changing times caused me to talk of sex equality and of comradeship in marriage, yet a marriage in which the wife did not "look up" to her husband seemed to me to lack the authentic emotion. The emotion which I really sought was not that of equal friendship, but that of adoration. For decades this unconscious craving alienated that only type of man that my developing conscious personality could really desire.

Thus the traditions around me and the religious emotions I had cherished prepared me not only to seek a master but to love and reverence him when discovered. If I should not be chosen in marriage I was equally well prepared to become the highly skilled and very devoted servant of some man in an office, treating him also as a god whose whims could never be wrong for me. It is the fate of hundreds of thousands of girls prepared as I was. But if I should be chosen in marriage by some man who was not quite god, I was ready with a cloud of ideals with which to enthrone him. . . .

. . . I would choose my own path in life and do whatever I found interesting whether it paid me anything in money or not. If necessary I could always earn money at odd jobs; had I not done so in school? It is a method I recommend to other Americans who wish to revert to the frontiersman's ideal of independence. It has given me a vivid life. . . .

An African American Woman:
Surviving the South

By the early years of the twentieth century, a system of rigid apartheid, or racial separation, ruled the lives of southern African Americans. Beyond its disastrous legal impact, it was accompanied by white threats, humiliations, and random violence that hung over the everyday lives of men and women. For mothers, sisters, and daughters, apartheid's insults and dangers were often of a different nature, less violent than those visited on men, but no less harmful.

The narrator here, who chose not to give her name, is a mother of three children and the wife of a doctor. But neither her intelligence, sterling character, nor class status provided any protection or legal way to confront her tormentors.

121

I was born in my father's own home, in his coveted white house with green blinds—his father's house in miniature. Here my father kept a small store, was burned out once and had other trials, but finally he had a large grocery store and feed store attached.

I have never lived in a rented house except for one year since I've been grown. I have never gone to a public school in my life, my parents preferring the teaching of a patient "New England schoolmarm" to the southern "poor white," who thought it little better than a disgrace to teach colored children—so much of a disgrace to teach colored children that she taught her pupils not to speak to her on the streets. My mother and her children never performed any labor outside of my father's and their own homes.

Today I have the same feeling my parents had. There is no sacrifice I would not make, no hardship I would not undergo rather than allow my daughters to go in service where they would be thrown constantly in contact with Southern white men, for they consider the colored girl their special prey.

It is commonly said that no girl or woman receives a certain kind of insult unless she invites it. That does not apply to a colored girl and woman in the South. The color of her face alone is sufficient invitation to the Southern white man—these same men who profess horror that a white gentleman can entertain a colored one at his table. Out of sight of their own women they are willing and anxious to entertain colored women in various ways. Few colored girls reach the age of sixteen without receiving advances from them—maybe from a young "upstart," and often from a man old enough to be their father, a white haired veteran of sin. Yes, and the men high in position, whose wives and daughters are leaders of society. I have had a clerk in a store hold my hand as I gave him the money for some purchase and utter some vile request; a shoe man to take liberties, a man in a crowd to place his hands on my person, others to follow me to my very door, a school director to assure me a position if I did his bidding.

It is true these particular men never insulted me but once; but there are others. I might write more along this line and worse things—how a white man of high standing will systematically set out to entrap a colored girl—but my identification would be assured in some quarters. My husband was also educated in an American Missionary Association school (God bless the name!), and after graduating took a course in medicine in another school. He has practiced medicine now for over ten years. By most frugal living and strict economy he saved enough to buy for a home a house of four rooms, which has since been increased to eight. Since our marriage we have bought and paid for two other places, which we rent. My husband's collections average one hundred dollars a month. We have an iron-bound rule that we must save at least fifty dollars a month. Some months we lay by more, but never less. We do not find this very hard to do with the rent from our places, and as I do all of my work except the washing and ironing.

We have three children two old enough for school. I try to be a good and useful neighbor and friend to those who will allow me. I would be contented and happy if I, an American citizen, could say as Axel Jarlson (the Swedish emigrant, whose story appeared in *The Independent* of

January 8th, 1903) says, "There are no aristocrats to push him down and say that he is not worthy because his father was poor." There are "aristocrats" to push me and mine down and say we are not worthy because we are colored. The Chinaman, Lee Chew, ends his article in *The Independent* of February 19th, 1903, by saying, "Under the circumstances how can I call this my home, and how can any one blame me if I take my money and go back to my village in China?"

Happy Chinaman! Fortunate Lee Chew! You can go back to your village and enjoy your money. This is my village, my home, yet I am outcast. See what an outcast! Not long since I visited a Southern city where the "Jim Crow" car law is enforced. I did not know of this law, and on boarding an electric car took the most convenient seat. The conductor yelled, "What do you mean? Niggers don't sit with white folks down here. You must have come from 'way up yonder. I'm not Roosevelt. We don't sit with niggers, much less eat with them." I was astonished and said, "I am a stranger and did not know of your law." His answer was: "Well, no back talk now; that's what I'm here for—to tell niggers their places when they don't know them."

Every white man, woman and child was in a titter of laughter by this time at what they considered the conductor's wit.

These Southern men and women, who pride themselves on their fine sense of feeling, had no feeling for my embarrassment and unmerited insult, and when I asked the conductor to stop the car that I might get off, one woman said in a loud voice, "These niggers get more impudent every day; she doesn't want to sit where she belongs."

No one of them thought that I was embarrassed, wounded and outraged by the loud, brutal talk of the conductor and the sneering, contemptuous expressions on their own faces. They considered me "impudent" when I only wanted to be alone that I might conquer my emotion. I was nervous and blinded by tears of mortification which will account for my second insult on this same day.

I walked downtown to attend to some business and had taken an elevator in an office building. I stood waiting for the elevator, and when the others, all of whom were white, got in I made a move to go in also, and the boy shut the cage door in my face. I thought the elevator was too crowded and waited; the same thing happened the second time. I would have walked up, but I was going to the fifth story, and my long walk downtown had tired me. The third time the elevator came down the boy pointed to sign and said, "I guess you can't read; but niggers don't ride in this elevator; we're white folks here, we are. Go to the back and you'll find an elevator for freight and niggers."

The occupants of the elevator also enjoyed themselves at my expense. This second insult in one day seemed more than I could bear. I could transact no business in my frame of mind, so I slowly took the long walk back to the suburbs of the city, where I was stopping.

My feelings were doubly crushed and in my heart, I fear, I rebelled not only against man but God. I have been humiliated and insulted often, but I never get used to it; it is new each time, and stings and hurts more and more.

The very first humiliation I received I remember very distinctly to this day. It was when I was very young. A little girl playmate said to me: "I like to come over to your house to play, we have such good times, and your ma has such good preserves; but don't you tell my ma I eat over here.

My ma says you all are nice, clean folks and she'd rather live by you than the white people we moved away from; for you don't borrow things. I know she would whip me if I ate with you, though, because you are colored, you know."

I was very angry and forgot she was my guest, but told her to go home and bring my ma's sugar home her ma borrowed, and the rice they were always wanting a cup of.

After she had gone home I threw myself upon the ground and cried, for I liked the little girl, and until then I did not know that being "colored" made a difference. I am not sure I knew anything about "colored." I was very young and I know now I had been shielded from all unpleasantness.

My mother got the whole story from me, but she couldn't satisfy me with her explanation—or, rather, lack of explanation. The little girl came often to play with me after that and we were little friends again, but we never had any more play dinners. I could not reconcile the fact that she and her people could borrow and eat our rice in their own house and not sit at my table and eat my mother's good, sweet preserves.

The second shock I received was horrible to me at the time. I had not gotten used to real horrible things then. The history of Christian men selling helpless men and women's children to far distant States was unknown to me; a number of men burning another chained to a post an impossibility, the whipping of a grown woman by a strong man unthought of. I was only a child, but I remember to this day what a shock I received. A young colored woman of a lovely disposition and character had just died. She was a teacher in the Sunday school I attended—a self-sacrificing, noble young woman who had been loved by many. Her coffin, room, hall and even the porch of her house were filled with flowers sent by her friends. There were lovely designs sent by the more prosperous and simple bouquets made by untrained, childish hands. I was on my way with my own last offering of love, when I was met by quite a number of white boys and girls. A girl of about fifteen years said to me, "More flowers for that dead nigger? I never saw such a to-do made over a dead nigger. Why, there must be thousands of roses alone in that house. I've been standing out here for hours and there has been a continual stream of niggers carrying flowers, and beautiful ones, too, and what makes me madder than anything else, those Yankee teachers carried flowers, too!" I, a little girl, with my heart full of sadness for the death of my friend, could make no answer to these big, heartless boys and girls, who threw stones after me as I ran from them.

When I reached home I could not talk for emotion. My mother was astonished when I found voice to tell her I was not crying because of the death of Miss W., but because I could not do something, anything, to avenge the insult to her dead body. I remember the strongest feeling I had was one of revenge. I wanted even to kill that particular girl or do something to hurt her. I was unhappy for days. I was told that they were heartless, but that I was even worse, and that Miss W. would be the first to condemn me could she speak.

That one encounter made a deep impression on my childish heart; it has been with me throughout the years. I have known real horrors since, but none left a greater impression on me.

My mother used to tell me if I always used nice manners it would make others show the same to me.

I believed that literally until I entered school, when the many encounters I had with white boys and girls going to and from school made me seriously doubt that goodness and manners were needed in this world. The white children I knew grew meaner as they grew older—more capable of saying things that cut and wound.

I was often told by white children whose parents rented houses: "You think you are white because your folks own their own home; but you ain't, you're a nigger just the same, and my pa says if he had his rights he would own niggers like you, and your home, too."

A child's feelings are easily wounded, and day after day I carried a sad heart. Today I carry a sad heart on account of my children. What is to become of them? The Southern whites dislike more and more the educated colored man. They hate the intelligent colored man who is accumulating something. The respectable, intelligent colored people are "carefully unknown"; their good traits and virtues are never mentioned. On the other hand, the ignorant and vicious are carefully known and all of their traits cried aloud.

In the natural order of things our children will be better educated than we, they will have our accumulations and their own. With the added dislike and hatred of the white man, I shudder to think of the outcome.

In this part of the country, where the Golden Rule is obsolete, the commandment, "Love thy neighbor as thyself" is forgotten; anything is possible.

I dread to see my children grow. I know not their fate. Where the white girl has one temptation, mine will have many. Where the white boy has every opportunity and protection, mine will have few opportunities and no protection. It does not matter how good or wise my children may be, they are colored. When I have said that, all is said. Everything is forgiven in the South but color.

An Irish American Cook

Supported by unshakable religious faith and close family ties, the millions of Irish immigrants who arrived early in the nineteenth century carried with them little more than a willingness to work and a few stitches of clothing. Protestants soon convinced themselves that America had opened the gates to its first white "enemy from within." Fleeing famine, oppression, and internal strife at home, the newcomers were hardly prepared for or interested in upsetting the social order. Thousands died on the nightmare voyage across the Atlantic, and the survivors left the gangplank desperate to recuperate, to find a home and a job. In crowded slums, they found scant

welcome, except from their own kind.

Men and youths were soon at work constructing canals, roads, sewers, tunnels, and railroads and later digging in mines or working in factories. Women who could leave their large families found jobs cleaning, in domestic service, and in industry. The Irish were thrust into competition with free African Americans for the least skilled, most undesirable, and lowest paid positions; in the South they were often considered more expendable than slaves. Poor health, malnutrition, and industrial accidents took their toll, and there was often not enough work to go around. By the 1850s the Irish third of New York City's population made up 69 percent of the paupers and 55 percent of those arrested.

Because they were poor, usually from rural areas, unskilled, uneducated, and particularly because they were the first large Catholic migration, the Irish were viewed with a mixture of loathing and fear. The Know-nothings, charging "The Negro is black outside; the Irishman is black inside," claimed they were part of a Papist conspiracy to bring down democratic institutions. Anti-Catholic propaganda became a thriving industry. In the 1890s the American Protective Association renewed fears of "Papists" by claiming Irish domination of city politics and pollution of representative government.

However, because of mounting numbers, urban Irish were beginning by then to command some political power with its accompanying economic advances. These changes from early to later nineteenth century are reflected in the reminiscences of an immigrant woman who rose from house servant to cook to owner of her own boarding house. Taken down by her former employer, identified only as "one of the best known literary women of America," her memoir was published, dialect intact, in 1905.

I don't know why anybody wants to hear my history. Nothing ever happened to me worth the tellin' except when my mother died . . . I was born nigh to Limavaddy; it's a pretty town close to Londonderry. We lived in a peat cabin, but it had a good thatched roof. Mother put on that roof. It isn't a woman's work, but she—was able for it.

There were sivin childher of us. John an' Matthew they went to Australia. Mother was layin' by for five yer to get their passage money. They went into the bush. We heard twice from thim and then no more. Not another word and that is forty year gone now—on account of them not reading and writing. Learning isn't cheap in them old countries as it is here, you see. I suppose they're dead now— John would be ninety now—and in heaven. They were honest men. My mother sent Joseph to Londonderry to larn the weaver's trade. My father he never was a steddy worker. He took to the drink early in life. My mother an' me an' Tilly we worked in the field for Squire Varney. Yes, plowin' and' seedin' and diggin'—any farm work he'd give us. We did men's work, but we didn't get men's pay. No, of course not. In winter we did lace work for a merchant in Londonderry. (Ann still can embroider beautifully.) It was pleasanter nor diggin' after my hands was fit for it. But it took two weeks every year to clean and soften my hands for the needle.

Pay was very small and the twins—that was Maria and Philip—they were too young to work with at all. What did we eat? Well, just potatoes. On Sundays, once a month, we'd maybe have a bit of flitch (cured pork). When the potatoes rotted—that was the hard times! Oh, yes, I mind the famine years. An' the cornmeal that the 'Mericans sent. The folk said they'd rather starve nor eat it. We didn't know how to cook it. Here I eat corn dodgers and fried mush fast enough.

Maria—she was one of the twins—she died the famine year of the typhus and—well, she sickened of the herbs and roots we eat—we had no potatoes.

Mother said when Maria died, "There's a curse on ould green Ireland and we'll get out of it." So we worked an' saved for four year an' we sent Tilly to America. She had always more head than me. She came to Philadelphia and got a place for general housework at Mrs. Bent's. Tilly got but two dollars a week, bein' a greenhorn. But she larned hand over hand, and Mrs. Bent kept no other help and laid out to teach her. She larned her to cook and bake and to wash and do up shirts—all American fashion. Then Tilly axed three dollars a week. Mother always said, "Don't ax a penny more than you're worth. But know your own vally and ax that."

She had no expenses and laid by money enough to bring me out before the year was gone. I sailed from Londonderry. The ship was a sailin' vessel, the "Mary Jane." The passage was $12. You brought your own eating, your tea an' meal, an' most had flitch. There was two big stoves that we cooked on. The steerage was a dirty place and we were eight weeks on the voyage—overtime three weeks. The food ran scarce, I tell you, but the captain gave some to us, and them that had plenty was king to the others. I've heard bad stories of things that went on in the steerage in them old times— smallpox and fevers and starvation and worse. But I saw nothing of them in my ship. The folks were decent and the captain was kind.

When I got there Mrs. Bent let Tilly keep me for two months to teach me—me bein' such a greenhorn. Of course I worked for her. Mr. Bent was foreman then in Spangler's big mills. After two months I got a place. They were nice appearing people enough, but the second day I found out they were Jews. I never had seen a Jew before, so I packed my bag and said to the lady, "I beg your pardon, ma'am, but I can't eat the bread of them as crucified the Saviour." "But," she said, "he was a Jew." So at that I put out. I couldn't hear such talk.

Then I got a place for general housework with Mrs. Carr. I got $2 till I learned to cook good, and then $3 and then $4. I was in that house as cook and nurse for twenty-two years. Mr. Bent came to be partner in the mills and got rich, and they moved into a big house in Germantown and kept a lot of help and Tilly was housekeeper. How did we keep our places so long? Well, I think me and Tilly was clean in our work and we was decent, and, of course, we was honest. Nobody living can say that one of the McNabbs ever wronged him of a cent. Mrs. Carr's interests was my interests. I took better care of her things than she did herself, and I loved the childher as if they was my own. She used to tell me my sin was I was stingy. I don't know. The McNabbs are no wasteful folk. I've worn one dress nine year and it looked decent then. Me and Tilly saved till we brought Joseph and Phil over, and they went into Mr. Bent's mills as weaver and spool boy and then they saved, and we all brought out my mother and father. We rented a little house in Kensington for them. There was a parlor in it and kitchen and two bedrooms and bathroom and marble doorstep, and a bell. We paid nine dollars a month rent. You'd pay double that now. It took all our savings to furnish it, but

Mrs. Bent and Mrs. Carr gave us lots of things to go in. To think of mother having a parlor and marble steps and a bell! They came on the old steamer "Indiana" and got here at night, and we had supper for them and the house all lighted up. Well, you ought to have seen mother's old face! I'll never forget that night if I live to be a hundred. After that mother took in boarders and Joseph and Phil was there. We all put every cent we earned into building associations. So Tilly owned a house when she died and I own this one now. Our ladies told us how to put the money so as to breed more, and we never spent a cent we could save. Joseph pushed on and got big wages and started a flour store, and Phil went to night school and got a place as clerk. He married a teacher in the Kensington public school. She was a showy miss! Silk dress and feathers in her hat!

Joseph did well in his flour store. He has a big one on Market Street now and lives in a pretty house out in West Philadelphia. He's one of the wardens in his church out there and his girls give teas and go to reading clubs.

But Phil is the one to go ahead! And his son, young Phil, is in politics and a member of councils.

It was Phil that coaxed me to give up work at Mrs. Carr's and to open my house for boarders here in Kensington. His wife didn't like to hear it said I was working in somebody's kitchen.

I heard that young Phil told some of his friends that he had a queer old aunt up in Kensington who played poor, but had a great store of money hoarded away. He shouldn't have told a story like that. But young folks will be young! I like the boy. He is certainly bringing the family into notice in the world. Last Sunday's paper had his picture and one of the young lady he is going to marry in New York. It called him the young millionaire McNabb. But I judge he's not that. He wanted to borrow the money I have laid by in the old bank at Walnut and Seventh the other day and said he'd double it in a week. No such work as that for me! But the boy certainly is a credit to the family!

Rocco Corresca: From Immigrant to Entrepreneur

Millions of Italians arrived in America around the turn of the century; more than two million came during the decade that ended in 1900. For many the countryside symbolized the oppression they had known in the old country, so they chose to live in cities. They crowded together near relatives or those from their region. Asked where they intended to settle, hundreds of thousands told American immigration authorities "Mulberry Street," the heart of New York City's Little Italy.

Though they came with a dream of quick wealth, most found they had exchanged one set of squalid circumstances for another. They struggled to learn a new language, new ways, and to find the promised opportunities. Starting at the bottom, they slowly made their way up, some faster than others. The story of Rocco Corresca may not be a "rags to riches" tale, but at nineteen he had learned a great deal and was on his way to success.

When I was a very small boy I lived in Italy in a large house with many other small boys, who were all dressed alike and were taken care of by some nuns. It was a good place, situated on the side of the mountain, where grapes were growing and melons and oranges and plums.

They taught us our letters and how to pray and say the catechism, and we worked in the fields during the middle of the day. We always had enough to eat and good beds to sleep in at night, and sometimes there were feast days, when we marched about wearing flowers.

Those were good times and they lasted till I was nearly eight years of age. Then an old man came and said he was my grandfather. He showed some papers and cried over me and said that the money had come at last and now he could take me to his beautiful home. He seemed very glad to see me and after they looked at his papers he took me away and we went to the big city—Naples. He kept talking about his beautiful house, but when we got there it was a dark cellar that he lived in and I did not like it at all. Very rich people were on the first floor. They had carriages and servants and music and plenty of good things to eat, but we were down below in the cellar and had nothing. There were four other boys in the cellar and the old man said they were all my brothers. All were larger than I and they beat me at first till one day Francisco said that they should not beat me any more, and then Paulo, who was the largest of all, fought him till Francisco drew a knife and gave him a cut. Then Paulo, too, got a knife and said that he would kill Francisco, but the old man knocked them both down with a stick and took their knives away and gave them beatings.

Each morning we boys all went out to beg and we begged all day near the churches and at night near the theaters, running to the carriages and opening the doors and then getting in the way of the people so that they had to give us money or walk over us. The old man often watched us and at night he took all the money except when we could hide something.

It was very hard in the wintertime for we had no shoes and we shivered a great deal. The old man said that we were no good, that we were ruining him, that we did not bring enough money. He told me that I was fat and that people would not give money to fat beggars. He beat me, too, because I didn't like to steal, as I had heard it was wrong.

"Ah!" said he, "that is what they taught you at that place, is it? To disobey your grandfather that fought with Garibaldi! That is a fine religion!"

The others all stole as well as begged, but I didn't like it and Francisco didn't like it either.

Then the old man said to me: "If you don't want to be a thief you can be a cripple. That is an easy life and they make a great deal of money."

I was frightened then, and that night heard him talking to one of the men that came to see him. He asked how much he would charge to make me a good cripple like those that crawl about the church. They had a dispute, but at last they agreed and the man said that I should be made so that people would shudder and give me plenty of money.

I was much frightened, but I did not make a sound and in the morning I went out to beg with Francisco. I said to him: "I am going to run away. I don't believe Tony is my grandfather. I don't believe that he fought for Garibaldi, and I don't want to be cripple, no matter how much money the people may give."

"Where will you go?" Franscisco asked me.

"I don't know," I said; "somewhere."

He thought awhile and then he said: "I will go, too."

So we ran away out of the city and begged from the country people as we went along. We came to a village down by the sea and a long way from Naples and there we found some fishermen and they took us aboard their boat. We were with them five years, and though it was a very hard life we liked it well because there was always plenty to eat. Fish do not keep long and those that we did not sell we ate.

The chief fisherman, whose name was Ciguciano, had a daughter, Teresa, who was very beautiful, and though she was two years younger than I, she could cook and keep house quite well. She was a kind, good girl and he was a good man. When we told him about the old man who told us he was our grandfather, the fisherman said he was an old rascal who should be in prison for life. Teresa cried much when she heard that he was going to make me a cripple. Ciguciano said that all the old man had taught us was wrong—that it was bad to beg, to steal, and to tell lies. He called in the priest and the priest said the same thing and was very angry at the old man in Naples, and he taught us to read and write in the evenings. He also taught us our duties to the church and said that the saints were good and would only help men to do good things, and that it was a wonder that lighting from heaven had not struck the old man dead when he knocked down the saint's figure.

We grew large and strong with the fisherman and he told us that we were getting too big for him, that he could not afford to pay us the money that we were worth. He was a fine, honest man—one in a thousand.

Now and then I had heard things about America—that it was a far off country where everybody was rich and that Italians went there and made plenty of money, so that they could return to Italy and live in pleasure ever after. One day I met a young man who pulled out a handful of gold and told me he had made that in America in a few days.

I said that I should like to go there, and he told me that if I went he would take care of me and see that I was safe. I told Francisco and he wanted to go, too. So we said good-bye to our good friends. Teresa cried and kissed us both, and the priest came and shook our hands and told us to be good men, and that no matter where we went God and his saints were always near us and that if we lived well we should all meet again in heaven. We cried, too, for it was our home, that place. Ciguciano gave us money and slapped us on the back and said that we should be great. But he felt bad, too, at seeing us go away after all that time.

The young man took us to a big ship and got us work away down where the fires are. We had to carry coal to the place where it could be thrown on the fires. Francisco and I were very sick from the great heat at first and lay on the coal for a long time, but they threw water on us and made us get up. We could not stand on our feet well, for everything was going around and we had no strength. We said that we wished we had stayed in Italy no matter how much gold there was in America. We could not eat for three days and could not do much work. Then we got better and sometimes we went up above and looked about. There was no land anywhere and we were much surprised. How could the people tell where to go when there was no land to steer by?

We were so long on the water that we began to think we should never get to America or that, perhaps, there was not any such place, but at last we saw land and came up to New York.

We were glad to get over without giving money, but I have heard since that we should have been paid for our work among the coal and that the young man who had sent us got money for it. We were all landed on an island and the bosses there said that Francisco and I must go back because we had not enough money, but a man named Bartolo came up and told them that we were brothers and he was our uncle and would take care of us. He bought two other men who swore that they knew us in Italy and that Bartolo was our uncle. I had never seen any of them before, but even then Bartolo might be my uncle, so I did not say anything. The bosses of the island let us go out with Bartolo after he had made the oath.

We came to Brooklyn to a wooden house in Adams Street that was full of Italians from Naples. Bartolo had a room on the third floor and there were fifteen men in the room, all boarding with Bartolo. He did the cooking on a stove in the middle of the room and there were beds all around the sides, one bed above another. It was very hot in the room, but we were soon asleep, for we were very tired.

The next morning, early, Bartolo told us to go out and

pick rags and get bottles. He gave us bags and hooks and showed us the ash barrels. On the streets where the fine houses are the people are very careless and put out good things, like mattresses and umbrellas, clothes, hats, and boots. We brought all these to Bartolo and he made them new again and sold them on the sidewalk; but mostly we brought rags and bones. The rags we had to wash in the backyard and then we hung them to dry on lines under the ceiling in our room. The bones we kept under the beds till Bartolo could find a man to buy them.

Most of the men in our room worked at digging the sewer. Bartolo got them the work and they paid him about one quarter of their wages. Then he charged them for board and he bought the clothes for them, too. So they got little money at all.

Bartolo was always saying that the rent of the room was so high that he could not make anything, but he was really making plenty. He was what they call a padrone and is now a very rich man. The men that were living with him had just come to the country and could not speak English. They had all been sent by the young man we met in Italy. Bartolo told us all that we must work for him and that if we did not the police would come and put us in prison.

He gave us very little money, and our clothes were some of those that were found on the street. Still we had enough to eat and we had meat quite often, which we never had in Italy. Bartolo got it from the butcher—the meat that he could not sell to the other people—but it was quite good meat. Bartolo cooked it in the pan while we all sat on our beds in the evening. Then he cut it into small bits and passed the pan around, saying:

"See what I do for you and yet you are not glad. I am

too kind a man, that is why I am so poor."

We were with Bartolo nearly a year, but some of our countrymen who had been in the place a long time said that Bartolo had no right to us and we could get work for a dollar and a half a day, which, when you make it *lire* (reckoned in the Italian currency) is very much. So we went away one day to Newark and got work on the street. Bartolo came after us and made a great noise, but the boss said that if he did not go away soon the police would have him. Then he went, saying that there was no justice in this country.

We paid a man five dollars each for getting us the work and we were with that boss for six months. He was Irish, but a good man and he gave us our money every Saturday night. We lived much better than with Bartolo, and when the work was done we each had nearly $200 saved. Plenty of the men spoke English and they taught us, and we taught them to read and write. That was at night, for we had a lamp in our room, and there were only five other men who lived in that room with us.

We got up at half-past five o'clock every morning and made coffee on the stove and had a breakfast of bread and cheese, onions, garlic, and red herrings. We went to work at seven o'clock and in the middle of the day we had soup and bread in a place where we got it for two cents a plate. In the evenings we had a good dinner with meat of some kind and potatoes. We got from the butcher the meat that other people would not buy because they said it was old, but they don't know what is good. We paid four or five cents a pound for it and it was the best, though I have heard of people paying sixteen cents a pound.

When the Newark boss told us that there was no more work Francisco and I talked about what we would do and we went back to Brooklyn to a saloon near Hamilton Ferry, where we got a job cleaning it out and slept in a little room upstairs. There was a bootblack named Michael on the corner and when I had time I helped him and learned the business. Francisco cooked the lunch in the saloon and he, too, worked for the bootblack and we were soon able to make the best polish.

Then we thought we would go into business and we got a basement on Hamilton Avenue, near the ferry, and put four chairs in it. We paid $75 for the chairs and all the other things. We had tables and looking glasses there and curtains. We took the papers that have the pictures in and made the place high toned. Outside we had a big sign that said

THE BEST SHINE FOR TEN CENTS

Men that did not want to pay ten cents could get a good shine for five cents, but it was not an oil shine. We had two boys helping us and paid each of them fifty cents a day. The rent of the place was $20 a month, so the expenses were very great, but we made money from the beginning. We slept in the basement, but got our meals in the saloon till we could put a stove in our place, and then Francisco cooked for us all. That would not do, though, because some of our customers said that they did not like to smell garlic and onions and red herrings. I thought that was strange, but we had to do what the customers said. So we got the woman who lived upstairs to give us our meals and paid her $1.50 a week each. She gave the boys soup in the middle of the day—five cents for two plates.

We remembered the priest, the friend of Ciguciano, and what he had said to us about religion, and as soon as we came to the country we began to go to the Italian church.

The priest we found here was a good man, but he asked the people for money for the church. The Italians did not like to give because they said it looked like buying religion. The priest says it is different here from Italy because all the churches there are what they call endowed, while here all they have is what the people give. Of course I and Francisco understand that, but the Italians who cannot read and write shake their hands and say that it is wrong for a priest to want money.

We had said that when we saved $1,000 each we would go back to Italy and buy a farm, but now that the time is coming we are so busy and making so much money that we think we will stay. We have opened another parlor near South Ferry, in New York. We have to pay $30 a month rent, but the business is very good. The boys in this place charge sixty cents a day because there is so much work.

At first we did not know much of this country, but by and by we learned. There are here plenty of Protestants who are heretics, but they have a religion, too. Many of the finest churches are Protestant, but they have no saints and no altars, which seems strange.

These people are without a king such as ours in Italy. It is what they call a Republic, as Garibaldi wanted, and every year in the fall the people vote. They wanted us to vote last fall, but we did not. A man came and said that he would get us made Americans for fifty cents and then we could get two dollars for our votes. I talked to some of our people and they told me that we should have to put a paper in a box telling who we wanted to govern us.

I went with five men to the court and when they asked me how long I had been in the country I told them two years.

146

Afterward my countrymen said I was a fool and would never learn politics. "You should have said you were five years here and then we would swear to it," was what they told me.

There are two kinds of people that vote here, Republicans and Democrats. I went to a Republican meeting and the man said that the Republicans want a Republic and the Democrats are against it. He said that Democrats are for a king whose name is (William Jennings) Bryan and who is an Irishman. There are some good Irishmen, but many of them insult Italians. They call us Dagoes. So I will be a Republican.

I like this country now and I don't see why we should have a king. Garibaldi didn't want a king and he was the greatest man that ever lived.

I and Francisco are to be Americans in three years. The court gave up papers and said we must wait and we must be able to read some things and tell who the ruler of the country is.

There are plenty of rich Italians here, men who a few years ago had nothing and now have so much money that they could not count all their dollars in a week. The richest ones go away from the other Italians and live with the Americans.

We have joined a club and have much pleasure in the evenings. The club has rooms down in Sackett Street and we meet many people and are learning new things all the time. We were very ignorant when we came here, but now we have learned much.

On Sundays we get a horse and carriage from the grocer and go down to Coney Island. We go to the theaters often and other evenings we go to the houses of our friends and play cards.

I am nineteen years of age now and have $700 saved. Francisco is twenty-one and has about $900. We shall open some more parlors soon. I know an Italian who was a bootblack ten years ago and now bosses bootblacks all over the city, who has so much money that if it was turned into gold it would weigh more than himself.

Francisco and I have a room to ourselves now and some people call us "swells." Francisco bought a gold watch with a gold chain as thick as his thumb. He is a very handsome fellow and I think he likes a young lady that he met at a picnic out at Ridgewood.

I often think of Ciguciano and Teresa. He is a good man, one in a thousand, and she was very beautiful. Maybe I shall write to them about coming to this country.

Sadie Frowne: A Jewish Sweatshop Operator at Sixteen

By the end of the nineteenth century the sweatshop was as much a fixed institution in urban America as the ghetto in which it was located. For young immigrant women, who had to spend as much time behind factory machines as in their homes, sweatshop labor was an experience they would never forget. Most sweatshops were located in dingy, dilapidated buildings. Operators were packed together without sufficient light or fresh air. The working day was long, the pay was a few dollars a week, and the rewards were few. Survival depended on satisfactions found outside working hours.

Sadie Frowne's story is probably one which many other young European women could have told.

When I was a little more than ten years of age my father died. He was a good man and a steady worker, and we never knew what it was to be hungry while he lived. After he died troubles began, for the rent of our shop was about $6 a month and then there were food and clothes to provide. We needed little, it is true, but even soup, black bread, and onions we could not always get.

We struggled along till I was nearly thirteen years of age and quite handy at housework and shop keeping, so far as I could learn them there. But we fell behind in the rent and mother kept thinking more and more that we should have to leave Poland and go across the sea to America where we heard it was much easier to make money. Mother wrote to aunt Fanny, who lived in New York, and told her how hard it was to live in Poland, and Aunt Fanny advised her to come and bring me. I was out at service at this time and mother thought she would leave me—as I had a good place—and come to this country alone, sending for me afterward. But Aunt Fanny would not hear of this. She said we should both come at once, and she went around among our relatives in New York and took up a subscription for our passage.

We came by steerage on a steamship in a very dark place that smelt dreadfully. There were hundreds of other people packed in with us, men, women, and children, and almost all of them were sick. It took us twelve days to cross the sea, and we thought we should die, but at last the voyage was over, and we came up and saw the beautiful bay and the big woman with the spikes on her head and the lamp that is lighted at night in her hand (Goddess of Liberty).

Sadie Frowne

Aunt Fanny and her husband met us at the gate of this country and were very good to us, and soon I had a place to live out (domestic servant), while my mother got work in a factory making white goods.

I was only a little over thirteen years of age and a greenhorn, so I received $9 a month and board and lodging, which I thought was doing well. Mother, who, as I have said, was very clever, made $9 a week on white goods, which means all sorts of underclothing, and is high class work.

But mother had a very gay disposition. She liked to go around and see everything, and friends took her about New York at night and she caught a bad cold and coughed and coughed. She really had hasty consumption, but she didn't know it, and I didn't know it, and she tried to keep on working, but it was no use. She had not the strength. Two doctors attended her, but they could do nothing, and at last she died and I was left alone. I had saved money while out at service, but mother's sickness and funeral swept it all away and now I had to begin all over again.

Aunt Fanny had always been anxious for me to get an education, as I did not know how to read or write, and she thought that was wrong. Schools are different in Poland from what they are in this country, and I was always too busy to learn to read and write. So when mother died I thought I would try to learn a trade and then I could go to school at night and learn to speak the English language well.

So I went to work in Allen Street (Manhattan) in what they call a sweatshop, making skirts by machine. I was new at the work and the foreman scolded me a great deal.

"Now, then," he would say, "this place is not for you to be looking around in. Attend to your work. That is what you have to do."

I did not know at first that you must not look around and talk, and I made many mistakes with the sewing, so that I was often called a "stupid animal." But I made $4 a week by working six days in the week. For there are two Sabbaths here—our own Sabbath, that comes on a Saturday, and the Christian Sabbath that comes on Sunday. It is against our law to work on our own Sabbath, so we work on their Sabbath.

In Poland I and my father and mother used to go to the synagogue on the Sabbath, but here the women don't go to the synagogue much, though the men do. They are shut up working hard all the week long and when the Sabbath comes they like to sleep long in bed and afterward they must go out where they can breathe the air. The rabbis are strict here, but not so strict as in the old country.

I lived at this time with a girl named Ella, who worked in the same factory and made $5 a week. We had the room all to ourselves, paying $1.50 a week for it, and doing light housekeeping. It was in Allen Street and the window looked out of the back, which was good, because there was an elevated railroad in front, and in summertime a great deal of dust and dirt came in at the front windows. We were on the fourth story and could see all that was going on in the back rooms of the houses behind us, and early in the morning the sun used to come in our window. We did our cooking on an oil stove, and lived well, as this list of our expenses for one week will show:

Sadie Frowne

Ella and Sadie for Food (One Week).

Tea $0.06
Cocoa .... .10
Bread and rolls .... .40
Canned vegetables .... .20
Potatoes .... .10
Milk .... .21
Fruit .... .20
Butter .... .15
Meat .... .60
Fish .... .15
Laundry .... .25
    Total $2.42
    Add rent 1.50
    Grand Total $3.92

Of course, we could have lived cheaper, but we are both fond of good things and felt that we could afford them.

We paid 18 cents for a half pound of tea so as to get it good, and it lasted us three weeks, because we had cocoa for breakfast. We paid 5 cents for six rolls and 5 cents for a loaf of bread, which was the best quality. Oatmeal cost us 10 cents for three and one-half pounds, and we often had it in the morning, or Indian meal porridge in the place of it, costing about the same. Half a dozen eggs cost about 13 cents on an average, and we could get all the meat we wanted for a good hearty meal for 20 cents—two pounds of chops, or a steak, or a bit of veal, or a neck of lamb—something like that. Fish included butter fish, porgies, codfish, and smelts, averaging about 8 cents a pound.

Some people who buy at the last of the market, when

the men with the carts want to go home, can get things very cheap, but they are likely to be stale, and we did not often do that with fish, fresh vegetables, fruit, milk, or meat. Things that kept well we did buy that way and got good bargains. I got thirty potatoes for 10 cents one time, though generally I could not get more than 15 of them for that amount. Tomatoes, onions, and cabbages, too, we bought that way and did well, and we found a factory where we could buy the finest broken crackers for 3 cents a pound, and another place where we got broken candy for 10 cents a pound. Our cooking was done on an oil stove, and the oil for the stove and the lamp cost us 10 cents a week.

It cost me $2 a week to live, and I had a dollar a week to spend on clothing and pleasure, and saved the other dollar. I went to night school, but it was hard work learning at first as I did not know much English.

Two years ago I came to this place, Brownsville, where so many people are, and where I have friends. I got work in a factory making underskirts—all sorts of cheap underskirts, like cotton and calico for the summer and woolen for the winter, but never the silk, satin, or velvet underskirts. I earned $4.50 a week and lived on $2 a week, the same as before.

I got a room in the house of some friends who lived near the factory. I pay $1 a week for the room and am allowed to do light housekeeping—that is, cook my meals in it. I get my own breakfast in the morning, just a cup of coffee and a roll, and at noontime I come home to dinner and take a plate of soup and a slice of bread with the lady of the house. My food for a week costs a dollar, just as it did in Allen Street, and I have the rest of my money to do as I like with. I am earning $5.50 a week now, and will probably get another increase soon.

It isn't piecework in our factory, but one is paid by the amount of work done just the same. So it is like piecework. All the hands get different amounts, some as low as $3.50 and some of the men as high as $16 a week. The factory is in the third story of a brick building. It is in a room twenty feet long and fourteen broad. There are fourteen machines in it. I and the daughter of the people with whom I live work two of these machines. The other operators are all men, some young and some old.

At first a few of the young men were rude. When they passed me they would touch my hair and talk about my eyes and my red cheeks, and make jokes. I cried and said that if they did not stop I would leave the place. The boss said that that should not be, that no one must annoy me. Some of the other men stood up for me, especially Henry, who said two or three times that he wanted to fight. Now the men all treat me very nicely. It was just that some of them did not know better, not being educated.

Henry is tall and dark, and he has a small mustache. His eyes are brown and large. He is pale and much educated, having been to school. He knows a great many things and has some money saved. I think nearly $400. He is not going to be in a sweatshop all the time, but will soon be in the real estate business, for a lawyer that knows him well has promised to open an office and pay him to manage it.

Henry has seen me home every night for a long time and makes love to me. He wants me to marry him, but I am not seventeen yet, and I think that is too young. He is only nineteen, so we can wait.

I have been to the fortune teller's three or four times, and she always tells me that though I have had such a lot of trouble I am to be very rich and happy. I believe her because she has told so many things that have come true. So I will keep on working in the factory for a time. Of course it is hard, but I would have to work hard even if I was married.

I get up at half-past five o'clock every morning and make myself a cup of coffee on the oil stove. I eat a bit of bread and perhaps some fruit and then go to work. Often I get there soon after six o'clock so as to be in good time, though the factory does not open till seven. I have heard that there is a sort of clock that calls you at the very time you want to get up, but I can't believe that because I don't see how the clock would know.

At seven o'clock we all sit down to our machines and the boss brings to each one the pile of work that he or she is to finish during the day, what they call in English their "stint." This pile is put down beside the machine and as soon as a skirt is done it is laid on the other side of the machine. Sometimes the work is not all finished by six o'clock and then the one who is behind must work overtime. Sometimes one is finished ahead of time and gets away at four or five o'clock, but generally we are not done till six o'clock.

The machines go like mad all day, because the faster you work the more money you get. Sometimes in my haste I get my finger caught and the needle goes right through it. It goes so quick, though, that it does not hurt much. I bind the finger up with a piece of cotton and go on working. We all have accidents like that. Where the needle goes through the nail it makes a sore finger, or where it splinters a bone it does much harm. Sometimes a finger has to come off. Generally, though, one can be cured by a salve.

All the time we are working the boss walks about examining the finished garments and making us do them over again if they are not just right. So we have to be careful as well as swift. But I am getting so good at the work that within a year I will be making $7 a week, and then I can save at least $3.50 a week. I have over $200 saved now.

The machines are all run by foot power, and at the end of the day one feels so weak that there is a great temptation to lie right down and sleep. But you must go out and get air, and have some pleasure. So instead of lying down I got out, generally with Henry. Sometimes we go to Coney Island, where there are good dancing places, and sometimes we go to Ulmer Park to picnics. I am very fond of dancing, and, in fact, all sorts of pleasure. I go to the theater quite often, and like those plays that make you cry a great deal. "The Two Orphans" is good. Last time I saw it I cried all night because of the hard times that the children had in the play. I am going to see it again when it comes here.

For the last two winters I have been going to night school at Public School *84* on Glenmore Avenue. I have learned reading, writing and arithmetic. I can read quite well in English now and I look at the newspapers every day. I read English books, too, sometimes. The last one that I read was "A Mad Marriage," by Charlotte Braeme. She's a grand writer and makes things just like real to you. You feel as if you were the poor girl yourself going to get married to a rich duke.

I am going back to night school again this winter. Plenty

of my friends go there. Some of the women in my class are more than forty years of age. Like me, they did not have a chance to learn anything in the old country. It is good to have an education; it makes you feel higher. Ignorant people are all low. People say now that I am clever and fine in conversation.

We have just finished a strike in our business. It spread all over and the United Brotherhood of Garment Workers was in it. That takes in the cloakmakers, coatmakers, and all the others. We struck for shorter hours, and after being out four weeks won the fight. We only have to work nine and a half hours a day and we get the same pay as before. So the union does good after all in spite of what some people say against it—that it just takes our money and does nothing. I pay 25 cents a month to the union, but I do not begrudge that because it is for our benefit. The next strike is going to be for a raise of wages, which we all ought to have. But though I belong to the union I am not a Socialist or an Anarchist. I don't know exactly what those things mean. There is a little expense for charity, too. If any worker is injured or sick we all give money to help.

Some of the women blame me very much because I spend so much money on clothes. They say that instead of a dollar a week I ought not to spend more than 25 cents a week on clothes, and that I should save the rest. But a girl must have clothes if she is to go into high society at Ulmer Park or Coney Island or the theater. Those who blame me are the old country people who have old-fashioned notions, but the people who have been here a long time know better. A girl who does not dress well is stuck in a corner, even if she is pretty, and Aunt Fanny says that I do just right to put on plenty of style.

I have many friends and we often have jolly parties. Many of the young men like to talk to me, but I don't go out with any except Henry.

Lately he has been urging me more and more to get married—but I think I'll wait.

Bernardo Vega: From Puerto Rico to New York

In 1898, the U.S. Army, acting on information provided by Puerto Rican freedom fighters, was able to defeat the Spanish occupying forces. When the United States claimed the island, Puerto Rico's leading figures voiced shock: "The voice of Puerto Rico has not been heard. Not even by way of formality were its inhabitants consulted as to whether they wanted to ask for, object to, or suggest any conditions bearing on their present or future political status. . . . The island and all its people were simply transferred from one sovereign power to another, just as a farm with all its equipment, houses, and animals is passed from one landlord to another."

Bernardo Vega

Born in 1885, when Puerto Rico was still ruled by Spain, Bernardo Vega was among millions who suddenly became "wards" of the United States. A proud, self-educated cigarworker, he joined the island's first large working class organization as a teenager, and at twenty he helped found the Puerto Rican Socialist Party.

In 1916 Vega sailed to New York, ready for hard work, new adventures, and political activity. His published autobiography is a mixture of diary, memoir, and history.

. . . From an early age I had worked as a cigar-roller in a tobacco factory. I had just turned thirty, and although it was not the first time I had left my hometown, never before had I put the shores of Puerto Rico behind me. I had been to the capital a few times. But now it meant going farther, to a strange and distant world. I hadn't the slightest idea what fate awaited me. . . .

. . . As soon as we were on the open sea and the boat started to pitch, the passengers went off to their cabins, most of them already half seasick. Not I. I stayed up on deck, lingering there until the island was lost from sight in the first shadows of nightfall.

The days passed peacefully. Sunrise of the first day and the passengers were already acting as though they belonged to one family. It was not long before we came to know each other's life stories. The topic of conversation, of course, was what lay ahead: life in New York. First savings would be for sending for close relatives. Years later the time would come to return home with pots of money. Everyone's mind was on that farm they'd be buying or the business they'd set up in town . . . All of us were building our own little castles in the sky.

When the fourth day dawned even those who had spent the whole trip cooped up in their cabins showed up on deck. As the boat entered the harbor the sky was clear and clean. The excitement grew the closer we got to the docks. We recognized the Statue of Liberty in the distance. Countless smaller boats were sailing about in the harbor. In front of us rose the imposing sight of skyscrapers — the same skyline we had admired so often on postcards. Many of the passengers had only heard talk of New York, and stood with their mouths open, spellbound . . . . Finally the *Coamo* docked at Hamilton Pier on Staten Island.

First to disembark were the passengers traveling first class — businessmen, well-to-do families, students. In second class, where I was, there were the emigrants, most of us *tabaqueros,* or cigar workers. We all boarded the ferry that crossed from Staten Island to lower Manhattan. We sighed as we set foot on solid ground. There, gaping before us, were the jaws of the iron dragon: the immense New York metropolis.

All of us new arrivals were well dressed. I mean, we had on our Sunday best. I myself was wearing a navy blue woolen suit (or *flus,* as they would say back home), a borsalino hat made of Italian straw, black shoes with pointy toes, a white vest, and a red tie. . . .

The Battery, which as I found out later is what they call the tip of lower Manhattan where our ferry from Staten Island docked, was also a port of call for all the elevated trains. The Second, Third, Sixth, and Ninth Avenue lines all met there. I entered the huge situation with Ambrosio

Fernández, who had come down to meet me at the dock. The noise of the trains was deafening, and I felt as if I was drowning in the crowd. Funny, but now that I was on land I started to feel seasick. People were rushing about every which way, not seeming to know exactly where they were headed. Now and then one of them would cast a mocking glance at the funny-looking travelers with their suitcases and other baggage. Finally there I was in a subway car, crushed by the mobs of passengers, kept afloat only by the confidence I felt in the presence of my friend.

The train snaked along at breakneck speed. I pretended to take note of everything, my eyes like the golden deuce in a deck of Spanish cards. The further along we moved, and as the dingy buildings filed past my view, all the visions I had of the gorgeous splendor of New York vanished. The skyscrapers seemed like tall gravestones. I wondered why, if the United States was so rich, as surely it was, did its biggest city look so grotesque? At the moment I sensed for the first time that people in New York could not possibly be as happy as we used to think they were back home in Cayey. . . .

On my first day in New York I didn't go out at all. There was a lot to talk about, and Ambrosio and I had lengthy conversations. I told him the latest from Puerto Rico, about our families and friends. He talked about the city, what life was like, what the chances were of finding a job . . . To put it mildly, an utterly dismal picture.

Ambrosio himself was out of work, which led me to ask myself, "Now, if Ambrosio is out of a job, and he's been here a while and isn't just a cigarworker but a silversmith and watchmaker to boot, then how am I ever going to find anything?" My mind began to cloud over with doubts;

frightening shadows fell over my immediate future. I dreaded the thought of finding myself out in the streets of such a big, inhospitable city. I paid the landlady a few weeks' rent in advance. Then, while continuing my conversation with Ambrosio, I took the further precautionary measure of sewing the money for my return to Puerto Rico into the lining of my jacket. I knew I only had a few months to find work before winter descended on us. If I didn't, I figured I'd send New York to the devil and haul anchor. . . .

. . . In those days you didn't need much to get by in New York. Potatoes were selling for a fraction of a cent a pound; eggs were fifteen cents a dozen; a pound of salt pork was going for twelve cents, and a prime steak for twenty cents. A nickel would buy a lot of vegetables. You could pick up a good suit for $10.00 With a nickel fare you could get anywhere in the city, and change from one line to another without having to pay more.

The next day I went out with Ambrosio to get to know New York. We headed for Fifth Avenue, where we got on a double-decker bus. It was the first time I had ever been on one of those strange contraptions! The tour was terrific. The bus went uptown, crossed over on 110th Street and made its way up Riverside Drive. At 135th Street we took Broadway up to 168th Street, and then St. Nicholas Avenue to 191st. From our comfortable seats on the upper deck we could soak in all the sights —the shiny store windows, then the mansions, and later on the gray panorama of the Hudson River. . . .

At the end of our tour, where we got off the bus, was a little park. We strolled through it, reading the inscriptions commemorating the War of Independence. We couldn't help noticing the young couples kissing right there in public. At first it upset me to witness such an embarrassing scene. But I quickly realized that our presence didn't matter to them. and Ambrosio confirmed my impression. What a difference between our customs back home and the behavior of Puerto Rican men and women in New York! . . .

On Park Avenue was an open-air market where you could buy things at low prices. Early in the morning the vendors would set up their stands on the sidewalk under the elevated train, and in the afternoon they would pack up their goods for the night. The marketplace was dirty and stank to high heaven . . . .

Many of the Jews who lived there in those days were recent immigrants, which made the whole area seem like a Tower of Babel. There were Sephardic Jews who spoke ancient Spanish or Portuguese; there were those from the Near East and from the Mediterranean, who spoke Italian, French, Provençal, Roumanian, Turkish, Arabic, or Greek. Many of them, in fact, could get along in five or even six languages. On makeshift shelves and display cases, hanging from walls and wire hangers, all kinds of goods were on display. You could buy everything from the simplest darning needle to a complete trousseau. For a quarter you could get a used pair of shoes and for two or three cents a bag of fruit or vegetables. . . .

At this time Harlem was a socialist stronghold. The Socialist Party had set up a large number of clubs in the neighborhood. Young working people would get together not only for political purposes but for cultural and sports activities and all kinds of parties. There were two major community centers organized by the party: the Harlem Terrace on 104th Street (a branch of the Rand School), and the Harlem Educational Center on 106th between Madison and Park. Other cultural societies and a large number of workers' cooperatives also worked out of these centers. Meetings and large indoor activities were held at the Park Palace, an auditorium with a large seating capacity. Outdoor public events were held at the corner of 110th Street and Fifth Avenue. All kinds of political, economic, social, and philosophical issues were discussed there; every night speakers aired their views, with the active participation of the public.

Housing in that growing neighborhood was for the most part owned by people who lived there. In many buildings the owners lived in one apartment and rented out the rest. There was still little or no exploitation of tenants by absentee landlords who had nothing to do with the community. The apartments were spacious and quite comfortable. They were well maintained precisely because the owners themselves lived in the buildings. Clearly, the Jewish people who lived in Harlem back then considered it their neighborhood and felt a sentimental attachment to it. Several generations had grown up there; they had their own schools, synagogues, and theaters. . . .

It was late, almost closing time, when we reached the León brothers' little cigar factory. Antonio, the eldest, harbored vivid memories of his little hometown of Cayey, which he had left so many years ago. His younger brothers, Pepín and Abelardo, had emigrated later but felt the same kind of nostalgia. There we were, pining for our distant homeland, when Ambrosio finally brought up the problem at hand: my pressing need for work. "Work, here?" the elder brother exclaimed. "This dump hardly provides for us!" Thus, my dream of rolling cigars in the León brothers' little factory was shattered. My tribulations in the iron

Tower of Babel had begun.

The following day Ambrosio and I began the challenging task of looking for work. We set out for the neighborhood where the bulk of the cigarworkers then lived: the blocks along Third Avenue, between 64th and 106th streets. Spread out over this large area were a lot of Puerto Ricans. There were also a lot in Chelsea, and up on the West Side of Manhattan, which is where the ones with money lived. . . .

In 1916 the Puerto Rican colony in New York amounted to about six thousand people, mostly *tabaqueros* and their families. The broader Spanish-speaking population was estimated at 16,000.

There were no notable color differences between the various pockets of Puerto Ricans. Especially in the section between 99th and 106th, there were quite a few black *paisanos*. Some of them, like Arturo Alfonso Schomburg, Agustín Vásquez, and Isidro Manzano, later moved up to the black North American neighborhood. As a rule, people lived in harmony in the Puerto Rican neighborhoods, and racial differences were of no concern.

That day we visited a good many cigar factories. The men on the job were friendly. Many of them even said they would help us out if we needed it. That's how cigarworkers were, the same in Puerto Rico as in Cuba, the same in Tampa as in New York. They had a strong sense of *compañerismo*— we were all brothers. But they couldn't make a place for us at the worktable of any factory. . . .

Meanwhile, thousands of Puerto Rican workers continued to land in New York. The apartments of those already here filled up with family, friends, and just anyone who was down and out. The number of Puerto Ricans climbed to 35,000. According to statistics kept by the International Cigarmakers' Union, there were over 4,500 Puerto Ricans enrolled in its various locals around the city. But the majority of the workers lacked a skilled trade, and made a large labor supply willing to take on the lowest paying jobs of New York.

No serious effort was made to organize the community and fight for its civil rights. The groups that did exist, as I have pointed out, had no other purpose than to organize dances. The only exception was the Club La Luz, located on the corner of Lenox and 120th Street, which in addition to dances would hold occasional cultural evenings. . . .

The first political campaign in New York in which Puerto Ricans participated was the Alfred Smith campaign of 1918. Around seven thousand Puerto Ricans registered to vote, the majority in the first and third electoral districts in Brooklyn. A major force behind the drive was the Club Democrático Puertorriqueño, the first organization of its kind inside the Democratic Party of the United States. It was founded and directed by two Puerto Ricans, J.V. Alonso and Joaquín Colón. . .

But the vast majority of Puerto Ricans in New York did not exercise their right to vote. It was no easy matter to go down to the Board of Elections and register. The officials would question the applicant in order to intimidate him. That kept a lot of Puerto Ricans away from the ballot box. Besides, most Puerto Ricans felt they had "nothing to get out of American politics," that "it didn't concern them." . . .

Neither of the political parties, Republican or Democrat, showed any real interest in winning the support of the Puerto Rican people. While their campaigns were in high gear, of course, some of their propaganda reached the Puerto Rican neighborhoods, but they did nothing to register voters. . . .

The drive to unionize Puerto Rican workers was facing similar problems. For the most part Puerto Ricans worked in nonunion shops. Sewing shops and restaurants, in particular, were filled with Puerto Ricans. But the unions in those lines of work didn't do a thing to recruit them. Furthermore, carpenters, bricklayers, tailors, and barbers who came from Puerto Rico were not admitted as members of the A.F. of L. unions.

In fact, not until the cigarmakers began to wage their union battles did unions in other trades show any interest in Puerto Rican workers. And that didn't happen until into the 1920s. Shortly before that, the first union to break through that barrier within labor, after the International Cigarmakers' Union, was the Furriers" Union.

Georgia Sharecroppers:
Slavery's New Clothes

For the African Americans of the South—about one-third of the region's population—life changed very little with the end of slavery. Their new freedom meant that they were no longer owned by individual whites. However, they were subject to rule by the white community as a whole and abuse by any individual. The system of southern justice, education, public welfare, and everything else was run by whites. Segregation was rigidly enforced, and white power extended far beyond economic, political, and legal spheres. A vast and complicated social code made Black men, women, and children subject to white whims and white pleasures.

Georgia Sharecroppers

The basis of this new slavery was the sharecropper system that bound African Americans to land owned by whites. Debts to the landlord kept people in peonage, unable to leave the job or move away. The story of this Georgia peon and his wife, dictated to a magazine writer who put it into a form suitable for publication, shows their lives were not their own, nor did they have any rights whites felt obliged to respect.

I am a negro and was born some time during the war in Elbert County, Ga., and I reckon by this time I must be a little over forty years old. My mother was not married when I was born, and I never knew who my father was or anything about him. Shortly after the war my mother died, and I was left to the care of my uncle. All this happened before I was eight years old, and so I can't remember very much about it. When I was about ten years old my uncle hired me out to Captain————. I had already learned how to plow, and was also a good hand at picking cotton. I was told that the Captain wanted me for his houseboy, and that later on he was going to train me to be his coachman. To be a coachman in those days was considered a post of honor, and, young as I was, I was glad of the chance. But I had not been at the Captain's a month before I was put to work on the farm, with some twenty or thirty other negroes—men, women, and children. From the beginning the boys had the same tasks as the men and women. There was no difference. We all worked hard during the week and would frolic on Saturday nights and often on Sundays. And everybody was happy. The men got $3 a week and the women

$2. I don't know what the children got. Every week my uncle collected my money for me, but it was very little of it that I ever saw. My uncle fed and clothed me, gave me a place to sleep, and allowed me ten or fifteen cents a week for "spending change," as he called it. I must have been seventeen or eighteen years old before I got tired of that arrangement, and felt that I was man enough to be working for myself and handling my own wages. The other boys about my age and size were "drawing" their own pay, and they used to laugh at me and call me "Baby" because my old uncle was always on hand to "draw" my pay. Worked up by these things, I made a break for Liberty. Unknown to my uncle or the Captain I went off to a neighboring plantation and hired myself out to another man. The new landlord agreed to give me forty cents a day and furnish me one meal. I thought that was doing fine. Bright and early one Monday morning I started for work, still not letting the others know anything about it. But they found it out before sundown. The Captain came over to the new place and brought some kind of officer of the law. The officer pulled out a long piece of paper from his pocket and read it to my new employer. When this was done I heard my new boss say:

"I beg your pardon, Captain. I didn't know this nigger was bound out to you, or I wouldn't have hired him."

"He certainly is bound out to me," said the Captain.

"He belongs to me until he is twenty-one, and I'm going to make him know his place."

So I was carried back to the Captain's. That night he made me strip off my clothing down to my waist, had me tied to a tree in his backyard, ordered his foreman to give me thirty lashes with a buggy whip across my bare back, and stood by until it was done. After that experience the Captain made me stay on his place night and day—but my uncle still continued to "draw" my money.

I was a man nearly grown before I knew how to count from one to one hundred. I was a man nearly grown before I ever saw a colored schoolteacher. I never went to school a day in my life. Today I can't write my own name, though I can read a little. I was a man nearly grown before I ever rode on a railroad train, and then I went on an excursion from Elberton to Athens. What was true of me was true of hundreds of other negroes around me—'way off there in the country, fifteen or twenty miles from the nearest town.

When I reached twenty-one the Captain told me I was a free man, but he urged me to stay with him. He said he would treat me right, and pay me as much as anybody else would. The Captain's son and I were about the same age, and the Captain said that, as he had owned my mother and uncle during slavery, and as his son didn't want me to leave them (since I had been with them so long), he wanted me to stay with the old family. And I stayed. I signed a contract—that is, I made my mark—for one year. The Captain was to give me $3.50 a week, and furnish me a little house on the plantation—a one-room log cabin similar to those used by his other laborers.

During that year I married Mandy. For several years Mandy had been the house-servant for the Captain, his wife, his son, and his three daughters, and they all seemed to think a good deal of her. As an evidence of their regard they gave us a suit of furniture, which cost about $25, and we set up housekeeping in one of the Captain's two-room shanties. I thought I was the biggest man in Georgia. Mandy

still kept her place in the "Big House" after our marriage.
We did so well for the first year, that I renewed my contract for the second year, and for the third, fourth, and
fifth year I did the same thing. Before the end of the fifth
year the Captain had died, and his son, who had married
some two or three years before, took charge of the plantation. Also, for two or three years, this son had been serving at Atlanta in some big office to which he had been
elected. I think it was in the Legislature or something of
that sort—anyhow, all the people called him Senator. At
the end of the fifth year the Senator suggested that I sign
up a contract for ten years; then he said, we wouldn't have
to fix up papers every year. I asked my wife about it; she
consented; and so I made a ten-year contract.

Not long afterward the Senator had a long, low shanty
built on his place. A great big chimney, with a wide, open
fireplace, was built at one end of it, and on each side of
the house, running lengthwise, there was a row of frames
or stalls just large enough to hold a single mattress. The
places for these mattresses were fixed one above the other;
so that there was a double row of these stalls or pens on
each side. They looked for all the world like stalls for horses.
Since then I have seen cabooses similarly arranged as sleeping quarters for railroad laborers. Nobody seemed to know
what the Senator was fixing for. All doubts were put aside
one bright day in April when about forty able-bodied
negroes, bound in iron chains, and some of them hand-
cuffed, were brought out to the Senator's farm in three big
wagons. They were quartered in the long, low shanty, and
it was afterward called the stockade. This was the beginning of the Senator's convict camp. These men were prisoners who had been leased by the Senator from the State

of Georgia at about $200 each per year, the state agreeing
to pay for guards and physicians, for necessary inspection,
for inquests, all rewards for escaped convicts, the costs of
litigation, and all other incidental camp expenses. When
I saw these men in shackles, and the guards with their guns,
I was scared nearly to death. I felt like running away, but
I didn't know where to go. And if there had been anyplace
to go to, I would have had to leave my wife and child behind. We free laborers held a meeting. We all wanted to
quit. We sent a man to tell the Senator about it. Word came
back that we were all under contract for ten years and that
the Senator would hold us to the letter of the contract, or
put us in chains and lock us up—the same as the other
prisoners. It was made plain to us by some white people
we talked to that in the contracts we had signed we had all
agreed to be locked up in a stockade at night or at any other
time that our employer saw fit; further, we learned that
we could not lawfully break our contract for any reason
and go and hire ourselves to somebody else without the
consent of our employer; and more than that, if we got
mad and ran away, we could be run down by bloodhounds,
arrested without process of law, and be returned to our
employer, who according to the contract, might beat us
brutally or administer any other kind of punishment that
he thought proper. In other words, we had sold ourselves
into slavery—and what could we do about it? The white
folks had all the courts, all the guns, all the hounds, all
the railroads, all the telegraph wires, all the newspapers,
all the money, and nearly all the land—and we had only
our ignorance, our poverty, and our empty hands. We
decided that the best thing to do was to shut our mouths,
say nothing, and go back to work. And most of us worked

side by side with those convicts during the remainder of the ten years.

But this first batch of convicts was only the beginning. Within six months another stockade was built, and twenty or thirty other convicts were brought to the plantation, among them six or eight women! The Senator had bought an additional thousand acres of land, and to his already large cotton plantation he added two great sawmills and went into the lumber business. Within two years the Senator had in all nearly *200* negroes working on his plantation—about half of them free laborers, so-called, and about half of them convicts. The only difference between the free laborers and the others was that the free laborers could come and go as they pleased at night—that is, they were not locked up at night, and were not, as a general thing, whipped for slight offenses.

The troubles of the free laborers began at the close of the ten-year period. To a man, they all wanted to quit when the time was up. To a man, they all refuse to sign new contracts—even for one year, not to say anything of ten years. And just when we thought that our bondage was at an end we found that it had really just begun. Two or three years before, or about a year and a half after the Senator had started his camp, he had established a large store, which was called the commissary. All of us free laborers were compelled to buy our supplies—foods, clothing, etc.—from that store. We never used any money in our dealings with the commissary, only tickets or orders, and we had a general settlement once each year in October. In this store we were charged all sorts of high prices for goods, because every year we would come out in debt to our employer. If not that, we seldom had more than $5 or $10 coming to us—

and that for a whole year's work. Well, at the close of the tenth year, when we kicked and meant to leave the Senator, he said to some of us with a smile (and I never will forget that smile—I can see it now):

"Boys, I'm sorry you're going to leave me. I hope you will do well in your new places—so well that you will be able to pay me the little balances which most of you owe me."

Word was sent out for all of us to meet him at the commissary at two o'clock. There he told us that, after we had signed what he called a written acknowledgment of our debts, we might go and look for new places. The storekeeper took us one by one and read to us statements of our accounts. According to the books there was no man of us who owed the Senator less than $100; some of us were put down for as much as $200. I owed $165, according to the bookkeeper. These debts were not accumulated during one year, but ran back for three and four years, so we were told—in spite of the fact that we understood that we had had a full settlement at the end of each year.

But no one of us would have dared to dispute a white man's word—oh, no; not in those days. Besides, we fellows didn't care anything about the amounts—we were after getting away; and we had been told that we might go, if we signed the acknowledgments. We would have signed anything, just to get away. So we stepped up, we did, and made our marks.

That same night we were rounded up by a constable and ten or twelve white men, who aided him, and we were locked up, every one of us, in one of the Senator's stockades. The next morning it was explained to us by the two guards appointed to watch us that, in the papers we had signed the day before, we had not only made the acknowledgment of our indebtedness, but that we had also agreed to work for the Senator unitl the debts were paid by hard labor. And from that day forward we were treated just like convicts. Really we had made ourselves lifetime slaves, or peons, as the laws called us. But, call it slavery, peonage, or what not, the truth is we lived in a hell on earth what time we spent in the Senator's peon camp.

I lived in that camp, as a peon, for nearly three years. My wife fared better than I did, as did the wives of some of the other negroes, because the white men about the camp used these unfortunate creatures as their mistresses. When I was first put in the stockade my wife was still kept for a while in the "Big House," but my little boy, who was only nine years old, was given away to a negro family across the river in South Carolina, and I never saw or heard of him after that. When I left the camp my wife had had two children for some one of the white bosses, and she was living in fairly good shape in a little house off to herself. But the poor negro women who were not in the class with my wife fared about as bad as the helpless negro men. Most of the time the women who were peons or convicts were compelled to wear men's clothes. Sometimes, when I have seen them dressed like men, and plowing or hoeing or hauling logs or working at the blacksmith's trade, just the same as men, my heart would bleed and my blood would boil, but I was powerless to raise a hand. It would have meant death on the spot to have said a word. Of the first six women brought to the camp, two of them gave birth to children after they had been there more than twelve months—and the babies had white men for their fathers!

The stockades in which we slept were, I believe, the filthiest places in the world. They were cesspools of nastiness. During the thirteen years that I was there I am willing to swear that a mattress was never moved after it had been brought there, except to turn it over once or twice a month. No sheets were used, only dark-colored blankets. Most of the men slept every night in the clothing that they had worked in all day. Some of the worst characters were made to sleep in chains. The doors were locked and barred each night, and tallow candles were the only lights allowed. Really the stockades were but little more than cow lots, horse stables, or hog pens. Strange to say, not a great number of these people died while I was there, tho a great many came away maimed and bruised and, in some cases, disabled for life. As far as I remember only about ten died during the last ten years that I was there, two of these being killed outright by the guards for trivial offenses.

It was a hard school that peon camp was, but I learned more there in a few short months by contact with those poor fellows from the outside world than ever I had known before. Most of what I learned was evil, and I now know that I should have been better off without the knowledge, but much of what I learned was helpful to me. Barring two or three severe and brutal whippings which I received, I got along very well, all things considered; but the system is damnable. A favorite way of whipping a man was to strap him down to a log, flat on his back, and spank him fifty or sixty times on his bare feet with a shingle or a huge piece of plank. When the man would get up with sore and blistered feet and an aching body, if he could not then keep up with the other men at work he would be strapped to the log again, this time face downward, and would be lashed with a buggy trace on his bare back. When a woman had to be whipped it was usually done in private, tho they would be compelled to fall down across a barrel or something of the kind and receive the licks on their backsides.

The working day on a peon farm begins with sunrise and ends when the sun goes down; or, in other words, the average peon works from ten to twelve hours each day, with one hour (from twelve o'clock to one o'clock) for dinner. Hot or cold, sun or rain, this is the rule. As to their meals, the laborers are divided up into squads or companies, just the same as soldiers in a great military camp would be. Two or three men in each stockade are appointed as cooks. From thirty to forty men report to each cook. In the warm months (or eight or nine months out of the year) the cooking is done on the outside, just behind the stockades; in the cold months the cooking is done inside the stockades. Each peon is provided with a great big tin cup, a flat tin pan, and two big tin spoons. No knives or forks are ever seen, except those used by the cooks. At mealtime the peons pass in single file before the cooks and hold out their pans and cups to receive their allowances. Cow peas (red or white, which when boiled turn black), fat bacon, and old-fashioned Georgia cornbread, baked in pones from one to two and three inches thick, make up the chief articles of food. Black coffee, black molasses, and brown sugar are also used abundantly. Once in a great while, on Sundays, biscuits would be made, but they would always be made from the kind of flour called "shorts." As a rule, breakfast consisted of coffee, fried bacon, cornbread, and sometimes molasses—and one "helping" of each was all that was allowed. Peas, boiled with huge hunks of fat bacon, and a hoe-cake, as big as a man's hand, usually answered for dinner. Sometimes this dinner bill of fare gave place to bacon and greens (collard or turnip) and

pot liquor. Tho we raised corn, potatoes and other vegetables, we never got a chance at such things unless we could
steal them and cook them secretly. Supper consisted of
coffee, fried bacon, and molasses. But, although the food
was limited to certain things, I am sure we all got a plenty
of the things allowed. As coarse as these things were, we
kept, as a rule, fat and sleek and as strong as mules. And
that, too, in spite of the fact that we had no special arrange-
ments for taking regular baths, and no very great effort
was made to keep us regularly in clean clothes. No tables
were used or allowed. In summer we would sit down on
the ground and eat our meals, and in winter we would sit
around inside the filthy stockades. Each man was his own
dishwasher—that is to say, each man was responsible for
the care of his pan and cup and spoons. My dishes got washed
about once a week!

Today, I am told, there are six or seven of these private
camps in Georgia—that is to say, camps where most of the
convicts are leased from the State of Georgia. But there
are hundreds and hundreds of farms all over the state where
negroes, and in some cases poor white folks, are held in
bondage on the ground that they are working out debts,
or where the contracts which they have made hold them
in a kind of perpetual bondage, because, under those contracts, they may not quit one employer and hire out to
another, except by and with the knowledge and consent of
the former employer. One of the usual ways to secure laborers for a large peonage camp is for the proprietor to
send out an agent to the little courts in the towns and villages, and where a man charged with some petty offense
has no friends or money the agent will urge him to plead
guilty, with the understanding that the agent will pay his

fine, and in that way save him from the disgrace of being sent to jail or the chain gang! For this high favor the man must sign beforehand a paper signifying his willingness to go to the farm and work out the amount of the fine imposed. When he reaches the farm he has to be fed and clothed, to be sure, and these things are charged up to his account. By the time he has worked out his first debt another is hanging over his head, and so on and so on, by a sort of endless chain, for an indefinite period, as in every case the indebtedness is arbitrarily arranged by the employer. In many cases it is very evident that the court officials are in collusion with the proprietors or agents, and that they divide the "graft" among themselves. As an example of this dickering among the whites, every year many convicts were brought to the Senator's camp from a certain county in south Georgia, 'way down in the turpentine district. The majority of these men were charged with adultery, which is an offense against the laws of the great and sovereign State of Georgia! Upon inquiry I learned that down in that county a number of negro lewd women were employed by certain white men to entice negro men into their houses; and then, on certain nights, at a given signal, when all was in readiness, raids would be made by the officers upon these houses, and the men would be arrested and charged with living in adultery. Nine out of ten of these men, so arrested and so charged, would find their way ultimately to some convict camp, and, as I said, many of them found their way every year to the Senator's camp while I was there. The low-down women were never punished in any way. On the contrary, I was told that they always seemed to stand in high favor with the sheriffs, constables, and other officers. There can be no room to doubt that they assisted very materially in furnishing laborers for the prison pens of Georgia, and the belief was general among the men that they were regularly paid for their work. I could tell more, but I've said enough to make anybody's heart sick. I am glad that the federal authorities are taking a hand in breaking up this great and terrible iniquity. It is, I know, widespread throughout Georgia and many other southern states. Since Judge Speer fired into the gang last November at Savannah, I notice that arrests have been made of seven men in three different sections of the state—all charged with holding men in peonage. Somewhere, somehow, a beginning of the end should be made.

But I didn't tell you how I got out. I didn't get out—they put me out. When I had served as a peon for nearly three years-—and you remember that they claimed that I owed them only $165—when I had served for nearly three years, one of the bosses came to me and said that my time was up. He happened to be the one who was said to be living with my wife. He gave me a new suit of overalls, which cost about seventy-five cents, took me in a buggy and carried me across the Broad River into South Carolina, set me down and told me to "git." I didn't have a cent of money, and I wasn't feeling well, but somehow I managed to get a move on me. I begged my way to Columbia. In two or three days I ran across a man looking for laborers to carry to Birmingham, and I joined his gang. I have been here in the Birmingham district since they released me, and I reckon I'll die either in a coal mine or an iron furnace. It don't make much difference which. Either is better than a Georgia peon camp. And a Georgia peon camp is hell itself!

Mike Trudics:
An Immigrant Is Enslaved

*By 1920, more than a million Hungarians had entered the
United States seeking a better life. Since most settled in the
Northeast or Middle West, few had the harrowing experience
of Mike Trudics. In 1906, Trudics joined other immigrants
who travelled to Savannah, Georgia, to work in a lumber
camp. They found themselves thrown back in time to the slave
era.*

*The South's landed aristocracy, who once enslaved Afri-
cans, now fashioned new chains with the crop lien, convict
labor, and sharecropping systems. Legislatures dutifully passed
poll taxes and other laws that segregated and disenfranchised
people of color. Former planters used this legislation and their*

economic power to also gain a whip hand over white employees. The South's labor system crushed unions, and again resembled an armed plantation of long hours and starvation wages.

Trudic's remarkably clear-eyed, poignant recollection of his childhood in the Austro-Hungarian empire, plus his battle against the new American slavery, are reminders of the price of liberty.

"I AM going to America!"

The words of my father startled us that night, for we were so quiet—out there two hours' walk from B_____. It was to us like saying he was going to be hung.

My father and mother were farmers. There were four of us children—two boys and two girls. John was ten, Annie twelve, I was seven and Mara sixteen.

We were at supper, but my father was not eating. "It is the best I could provide," my mother said, thinking it was the food.

"It is not that," he said. Then he spoke of America, and we all looked at him with our mouths wide open.

Mother stopped eating and we children had more black bread that night than we could eat. After supper we gathered closely around the open fire. All of us got very close to father. Annie sat on his knee, I sat on the hearth with my arms around his leg, while John and Mara leaned their heads against him. Mother rocked and rocked, looking with big eyes into the fire all the time.

"Even if I owned a farm," father said, "what difference

would it make? I need a mule, I need a plow—I need many tools. It breaks my back to do a mule's work, and the best I can do brings but black bread, and not even enough of that."

I did not understand what all this meant; I only knew in a dim kind of way that something had gone wrong. My father was a different man to me. My mother, too, looked strange. Her eyes were large, and she would look a long time at one place.

Our hearts were heavy. They were heaviest at night, but during the day I saw my mother weep and kneel for long periods at the ikon. We had all been baptized in the Russian Church, and one day the priest came and said a blessing for my father.

"Yes, yes," my father said when the priest was gone, "prayers are all right, but they are not black bread. They do not pay the rent. The priest says prayers and I sweat and give my blood; that is different."

My mother made the sign of the cross and said, "God is good! God is good!"

When my father picked us up one by one to say goodbye, he kissed us many times. Then, to please my mother, he went over to the ikon in the corner, and dropping on his knees crossed himself. We all sobbed aloud.

Nikof Jaros, our neighbor who lived alone, came with his mule to take father and his box; but we all cried so loud that he had to take us all. The journey was a fine holiday for us and we forgot our trouble on the way. It was different coming back.

"In two months," my father said, "I will send for you." We hugged him tight and hollered, though there were crowds of people around. My mother still wept quietly and said, "God is good! God is good!"

"America is great," Nikof told us on the way home. "It is not a land of fat priests and skinny people. Everybody has plenty and every man is a lawyer. The people make whatever laws they like."

We thought Nikof was very wise—except when he was drunk.

We were very lonely. When the wood fire burned brightly on the hearth at night we all sat around it just thinking, thinking about father. Mother used to gather us around the ikon every night and make us say our prayers. John cut a nick in the door-post for every day the ship was at sea. One day, when the posts on each side of the door were covered with nicks, a letter with George Washington's picture on it came to B———. John got it. None of us could read it, but the feel of it was very nice and we all handled it in turn. We handled it over and over. Mother wept over it before she knew what was in it. Nikof was sent for—he can read. He came at night. It was a great night for us. We believed more than ever that Nikof was really a great man. He read the letter over to us. Indeed he read it so often that we could all repeat it by heart. For so much paper there seemed to be very little communication. It just said father was well and making a fortune very fast.

A week afterward the priest came to our house, and after telling him the good news, mother gave him the letter. We all watched his round, red face. There were so many expressions on it in a minute.

"Nikof is a liar!" he said. "Jan Trudics is dead! This letter is from a friend of his who says Jan walked the streets of New York looking for work until his feet were blistered.

It says that at the end of a week he was taken ill and died. It says he died of a broken heart!"

My mother began to cry, and that started all of us.

"Be quiet!" The old priest said sternly. "God will be a father to the orphans. He will succor the widow in her distress!" But we cried all the louder. That night we gathered closely about mother.

John brought in extra wood and we sat silently by the fire watching the red flames as they leaped up the old chimney. Mother's face made us all cry. It was so pinched. Her lips were white and her eyes were sunken deep into her head, and for long hours she just looked steadily into the fire. We cried until one after another we went to sleep, and mother carried us to our bed in a corner.

Mother pined and prayed and spent much time before the ikon. As the days passed there was less and less black bread. Nikof came often, and always brought something to eat. He seemed to know our affairs, though nobody ever told him. We liked him very much even though he did read the letter backward. "For stupid peasants," Nikof said, "knowledge is a great curse. The less we know, the less we need." When he cursed the old priest only one of us agreed with him—that was Mara.

A year from the time my father went away my mother was in her grave, and the old priest and the doctor said that she, too, died from a broken heart. When we gathered around the fire again, we were a quiet, sorrowful lot. Nikof came and sat up late with us. He chopped plenty of wood and made some cakes with his own hands. He told us plenty of stories—good stories about God and another world than this, where father and mother were. "There,"

he said, "we will all be spirits and we will have no stomachs at all."

"The priest does not say we shall have no stomachs," said
Mara.

"I know," Nikof said. "He is always making me out a liar—
he is all stomach, the old—"

Mara put her hand on Nikof's mouth and stopped him.

Some kind-hearted folks in B——— took John and
somebody took Annie. Mara and I were unprovided for.
One day Nikof hitched up his old mule and took us for a
ride. It was a long ride to the city, and Nikof and Mara
seemed to have all the conversation to themselves. But I
was glad of the ride anyway. And when we drove up to the
priest's door Nikof let me mind the mule while he and Mara
went inside. When they came out again Mara's face had a
different look. She looked as she did before father went away,
and I was very glad. I thought she had gone for a blessing
to the old priest, but Nikof said:

"That is not it at all. We have just got married."

I was very glad. Nikof took us to his own little farm a
few miles from our old home and we lived there happily
with him for a year. In a year Nikof got drunk just once. It
was when he was with a soldier in the city. They got too
much brandy and on the way home lay down in the snow.
They found the soldier dead and Nikof had both his legs
sawed off later.

I was taken to the city and given away. I was nine at the
time. I did not see Mara for years after that, though we
were only two hours' walk apart. One day they told me that
Mara had gone crazy and that she had left Nikof.

At fifteen I became apprenticed to a molder. It was a
place where were made cornices—cornices of tin and zinc

for churches and other fine buildings. I stayed there until I was twenty years of age. Then I worked at a number of things—at times a common laborer and again as a teamster.

After I was twenty I attended meetings of different kinds. I heard a lecture once on America by a man who had gone there as a poor emigrant and returned a rich man. He said America was a country of magic. He told of wonderful things men had done, but all the time I was thinking, thinking of my father, of his blistered feet and broken heart. It was not his talk, however, but a book by Louis Kossuth that stirred me up to go to America. It took me nearly a year to get enough money to come. I about half starved myself to do it.

It was in May, 1906, that I came to New York. I was then twenty-four years of age. It certainly did look wonderful from the ship! A well dressed man who spoke our language told us that the big iron woman in the harbor was a goddess that gave out liberty freely and without cost to everybody. He said the thing in her hand that looked like a broom was light—that it was to give us light and liberty too. I thought he talked like Nikof Jaros. Especially when he told us a man could stand inside the broom.

I thought the rich people lived in the big, tall houses, but he said that was a mistake; they just did business there. He said they lived in palaces that would make our eyes bulge out if we could see them.

At Ellis Island they put my life in a book and asked me a lot of funny questions. Did I believe in law? Was I in favor of government? Etc.

When I got away from them I found my way to my mother's brother on East Third street, near the river. My uncle was a brass polisher, but although he had been many years in New York, he had not performed any miracle; he had not seen any magic. He had an ordinary kind of a job that he held in an ordinary kind of a way for a number of years. I expected, of course, to find him rich, but he laughed loudly at that, for he had that idea himself when he first landed.

The man my uncle lived with was an old friend of my father's. He gave me a corner in one of the two rooms. It was a good corner and I was happy in it.

Of course I looked around for the dwellings that were to make my eyes bulge out of my head. I saw only tenements, however. Maybe they were barracks. I was much bewildered by these big houses. They looked like big stone caves and the people were so crowded that they knocked each other about the streets. Indeed they rushed along as if they were crazy.

I got a job with my uncle at $10 a week. That seemed a very big price to get for my labor, but the price of board was so many times larger than it was in the old country. However, I was getting along very well until the factory was destroyed by fire. Then I had the experience of looking for work. It was easy as long as I had money to pay my board, but when my money had gone and I was dependent on my uncle and my father's old friend, I felt it very keenly indeed. I kept going, going, going, until my legs were very tired. Then a feeling of home-sickness came over me, and I came to the place where my father had been—I mean the condition he had experienced eighteen years ago. But I was young and had no one dependent upon me. I dreaded debt, and I would rather be beaten than called a loafer. Yet work I could not get. I ran up a board bill of $2. That worried me and I determined to go away and fight it out alone. I wrote a note and left it on the table. I promised to pay the bill as soon as I got work and asked them not to think unkindly of me because I left in a hurry.

I met on the street a Hungarian who had arrived on the same ship. He told me of an agency where they wanted men. So together we went there. The names of the employment people were Franks & Miller. My friend and I did not have much clothing, but what I had was good and strong.

"You will work in a sawmill," they said, "and you will get $1.50 a day and your food."

That seemed all right and I counted up on paper how much I could save in six months. It seemed big—very big. All my fellow laborers seemed pleased. I thought of my father: how fortunate for him if he had found an agency like this!

The railroad fare was $18. That, of course, was paid for us by the agency, so they said, and we were to pay it back at the rate of $3 a month, and if we liked the work and stayed for so many months we would not have to pay it at all.

We looked at each other with wide open eyes.

"You bet I'm going to stay three months!" said Lanniger, a Hungarian friend I had met on the voyage. I determined to do so too.

Eighteen dollars seemed a lot to save by just holding on to a fine job, and the very thought of $45 a month made me laugh with joy. I imagined myself going back to Hungary rich!

We looked a queer lot as we went to the boat. There were so many nations represented, and we were so differently dressed.

I had good, stout boots and woolen socks; a fine cap; a

cotton shirt with cotton collar and a bright new tie. My clothes were strong and whole.

I was one of a gang. There were all sorts of men in it. We whipped from New York to Savannah by boat and from there to Lockhart by rail. A young man whom they called "doctor" met us at Savannah. I liked the look of him. He had large eyes and a fine, kindly face. It was July 18th, 1906, when we arrived at Lockhart. The first thing we saw was an immense saw-mill.

"This is our place," said Lanniger.

"Good!" I said. "I am glad to be so near a good, long job. I am tired out."

But we stayed there only an hour. Certain men were picked out to stay and others were ordered on board a little engine. I was of the latter, and soon we were crashing noisily through the forest to the camp. The journey was about seven miles. A sort of dread seized me as we tore along. I was filled with suspicion, but I did not tell anybody. The camp was a train of box cars and around the camps were a lot of wooden sheds, stables and shops. My contract called for work in a saw-mill. I got enough courage to speak up.

"My contract says saw-mill," I said.

Gallagher, the boss, was chewing a toothpick while he looked us over. He paid no attention, but just looked at me as if I were crazy.

"My contract"—I would have said more, but he waved me aside.

Gallagher is a stout little man with a revolver sticking out of his hip pocket, and before we were an hour in the camp we heard some examples of his fearful profanity.

"Put him on the railroad, Charlie," he said to the underboss. The men standing around laughed.

The food in the camp was very good and there was plenty of it. We sat down to meals in a box car around a long table. The table was covered with good things—pork, meat, potatoes, bread and cake. We had tin cups and tin dishes.

The bunks in the car were too close together and too many men slept in them, I could not rest easily. My mind was disturbed.

The hours of labor were from six to six.

The work in the woods sawing logs was hot—too hot and too heavy for me. I learned that the pay was $1 a day. I told them how the agency had told me that the pay was $1.50 a day and food. They smiled at that.

So here we were, out in a wild place, helpless and at the mercy of men who laughed at contracts and out of whose hip pockets bulged revolvers. I did a lot of thinking. I talked to Lanniger.

"I'll run the first chance I get!" Lanniger said.

"I won't wait for a chance," I replied. "I'll make one and go!"

Next day before it was daylight I left the camp—not knowing where I was going. I knew the lumber company was big and powerful and that I was less to them than a log of wood. I was afraid most of the time. I walked all the forenoon, not knowing where I was going. Every time I saw any one coming I hid in the woods. About noon time I saw some men coming along the road in a buggy. When they approached I knew Gallagher. Sandor, the Hungarian interpreter, was there, as was also Dr. Grace, the camp veterinarian. They had three bloodhounds with them.

"There's the son of a —," I heard him say as he leaped from the buggy and rushed at me.

The doctor was at his heels in a moment and seized me with his right hand, while he pointed a revolver at me with his left. Gallagher had a horse-whip and at once struck me on the hips. He coiled the lash around my back at every stroke. Sandor sat in the buggy. I screamed in Hungarian to him, but he dared not move or interfere. After a dozen strokes my back was raw and the lashes sank into the bloody ruts of their predecessors. It made me howl with pain. Gallagher whipped me until he was exhausted. Then they drove me like a steer at the point of revolver along the road toward Lockhart. I appealed in my native tongue again, but Sandor told me that just as surely as I ever attempted to run away again, they would kill me. I believed him. In the woods they can do anything they please, and no one can see them but God.

When we arrived at Lockhart, where the sawmill is, I again protested and showed my contract, for I thought I was in a town where perhaps there might be some law or civilization. But I soon discovered the kind of law lumbermen are accustomed to. Gallagher whipped me a second time—whipped me until my shirt was glued to my back with my blood. Then they tied me in the buggy by the arms and legs, and with a drawn revolver and yelping bloodhounds, we drove away through the woods to the camp. That night armed guards kept watch over the laborers in the box cars. Hardly a day passed after that without some one being run down by the bosses or the bloodhounds and returned and whipped. There were some ghastly beatings in the broad daylight, but most of it was done in the barn.

In the daytime I had no time to think, but at night as I lay awake in my bunk, I made up my mind that not only most men, but most books also, were liars. I thought of that first picture of Washington on our letter at home; how Nikof thrilled us all with interest in it. I remembered the burning words of Kossuth on his impressions of America. But here I am with my own feet on American soil. I hear with my own ears; I see with my own eyes; I feel with my own feelings the brutality.

The bosses of the lumber company were put on trial and we told our stories; at least those of us who were still remaining. Of all the things that mixed my thinking in America, nothing was so strange as to find that the bosses who were indicted for holding us in peonage could go out free on bail, while we, the laborers, who had been flogged and beaten and robbed, should be kept in jail because we had neither money nor friends. We were well treated, of course, but at first I felt like a criminal. I am not sorry now for that jail experience, for I learned more about America than I would have learned in a year in a night school.

Foster was an American. He had fought in the Spanish-American War. He told us about graft and politics. "To get on," he said, "you must be a grafter here. Honesty never pays. A tip to the lumber bosses that we would lie on the stand and we would be out of here by noontime."

Lanniger was with me. We laughed at the queer ideas of free men. We talked all day, every day.

"Is Gallagher a grafter?" I asked.

"No," Foster said. "He is just a common slave-driver."

"Do they flog men everywhere in this country?"

"No, just down here in the South where they used to flog niggers. Thirty thousand laborers are sent South every year. They come down to mines, they fill the camps of all kinds, but they never stay."

"Why not?" I asked.

"Well, for the same reason that none of us will stay—small pay and nothing to see."

I learned much English from Foster, especially slang. When conversation was dry I got very tired of iron bars and jingling keys. They hurt my mind.

"Say, Mike," Foster said, "you're dead in luck to be here. In the stockades you'd dig five tons of coal a day, and for a lump of black rock found in your coal they'd flog you raw. Over there across the way in the city prison you'd be squeezed in an iron cage seven by three feet"—he measured it off for me—"and you'd be forced to sleep in the excrements of the hobos that were there ahead of you. I've been there; I know."

Then I was more content with the county jail. The trial came off in November, 1906, and we went every day for weeks to the big Government building. In the trial I learned that there was law in America, but its benefits to the poor were accidental. I was glad to see Gallagher get fifteen months in prison. I think he deserved much more. But Foster said he'd never serve a day. I asked him why, but he merely said, "Graft."

Old Jordoneff and I got work on Fort Pickens in the Gulf of Mexico as laborers in the repair of forts, where I am working now. We have very good pay—$1.25 a day and our board.

The boss is a gentleman.

We work eight hours a day and get a day off every two weeks. But the men we work for, even the under-bosses, are humane and kind. Therefore we do far more work and far better work, and work is a pleasure.

Shall I become a citizen?

Why should I?

Ah-nen-la-de-ni:
A Mohawk Receives a
White Education

With the arrival of Europeans in the 1500s, Native Americans became the first victims of racism on the American continents. By the early twentieth century, proud Indian nations had been overwhelmed militarily, forced from ancestral lands and reduced to a shadow existence as "wards" of their former foes.

The victors, however, not content with their triumph, demanded that the survivors reject ancient cultures and deities, embrace Christianity and the idea of private property, and even surrender their children to white education. Indian children were whisked off to distant schools where they were compelled to adopt a new outlook, dress, and civilization.

Ah-nen-la-de-ni

Ah-nen-la-de-ni, whose name means "Turning Crowd,"
was given this choice as a boy, and his reaction provides a
glimpse of what it meant to make a forced march between
two worlds.

I was born in Governeur Village, New York, in April, 1879,
during one of the periodical wanderings of my family. My
father was a pure-blooded Indian of the Mohawk tribe of
the Six Nations, and our home was in the St. Regis reservation in Franklin County, New York, but we were frequently away from that place because my father was an
Indian medicine man, who made frequent journeys, taking his family with him and selling his pills and physics in
various towns along the borderline between Canada and
the United States.

My father was rather a striking figure. His hair was long
and black, and he wore a long Prince Albert coat while in
the winter quarters, and Indian costume, fringed and
beaded, while in the tent. His medicines were put up in pill
boxes and labeled bottles, and were the results of knowledge that had been handed down through many generations in our tribe.

My brother and I also wore long hair, and were strange
enough in appearance to attract attention from the white
people about us, but mother kept us away from them as
much as possible.

My father was not only a doctor, but also a trapper,
fisherman, farmer, and basket-maker.

The reservation in Franklin county is a very beautiful

place, fronting on the main St. Lawrence River. On this reservation we had our permanent home in a log house surrounded by land, on which we planted corn, potatoes, and such other vegetables as suited our fancies. The house was more than fifty years old.

The woods provided my father and grandmother with their herbs and roots, and they gathered there the materials for basket-making. We were generally on the reservation in early spring, planting, fishing, basket-making, gathering herbs and making medicine, and then in the fall, when our little crop was brought in, we would depart on our tour of the white man's towns and cities, camping in a tent on the outskirts of some place, selling our wares, which included bead work that mother and grandmother were clever at making, and moving on as the fancy took us until cold weather came, when my father would generally build a little log house in some wood, plastering the chinks with moss and clay, and there we would abide, warm amid ice and snow, till it was time to go to the reservation again.

One might imagine that with such a great variety of occupations we would soon become rich—especially as we raised much of our own food and seldom had any rent to pay—but this was not the case. I do not know how much my father charged for his treatment of sick people, but his prices were probably moderate, and as to our trade in baskets, furs and bead work, we were not any better business people than Indians generally.

Nevertheless, it was a happy life that we led, and lack of money troubled us little. We were healthy and our wants were few.

Father did not always take his family with him on his expeditions, and as I grew older I passed a good deal of time on the reservation. Here, tho the people farmed and dressed somewhat after the fashion of the white man, they still kept up their ancient tribal ceremonies, laws, and customs, and preserved their language. The general government was in the hands of twelve chiefs, elected for life on account of supposed merit and ability.

There were four Indian day schools on the reservation, all taught by young white women. I sometimes went to one of these, but learned practically nothing. The teachers did not understand our language, and we knew nothing of theirs, so much progress was not possible.

Our lessons consisted of learning to repeat all the English words in the books that were given us. Thus, after a time, some of us, myself included, became able to pronounce all the words in the fifth and sixth readers, and took great pride in the exercise. But we did not know what any of the words meant.

Our arithmetic stopped at simple numeration, and the only other exercise we had was in writing, which, with us, resolved itself into a contest of speed without regard to the form of letters.

The Indian parents were disgusted with the schools, and did not urge their children to attend, and when the boys and girls did go of their own free will it was more for sociability and curiosity than from a desire to learn. Many of the boys and girls were so large that the teachers could not preserve discipline, and we spent much of our time in the school drawing pictures of each other and the teacher, and exchanging in our own language such remarks as led to a great deal of fighting when we regained the open air. Often boys went home with their clothing torn off them in these fights.

Under the circumstances, it is not strange that the attendance at these schools was poor and irregular, and that on many days the teachers sat alone in the school-house because there were no scholars. Since that time a great change has taken place, and there are now good schools on the reservation.

I was an official of one of the schools, to the extent that I chopped wood for it, but I did not often attend its sessions, and when I was thirteen years of age, and had been nominally a pupil of the school for six years, I was still so ignorant of English that I only knew one sentence, which was common property among us alleged pupils: "Please, ma'am, can I go out?" Pronounced: "Peezumgannigowout!"

When I was thirteen a great change occurred, for the honey-tongued agent of a new government-contract Indian school appeared on the reservation, drumming up boys and girls for his institution. He made a great impression by going from house to house and describing, through an interpreter, all the glories and luxuries of the new place, the good food and teaching, the fine uniforms, the playground and its sports and toys.

All that a wild Indian boy had to do, according to the agent, was to attend this school for a year or two, and he was sure to emerge therefrom with all the knowledge and skill of the white man.

My father was away from the reservation at the time of the agent's arrival, but mother and grandmother heard him with growing wonder and interest, as I did myself, and we finally decided that I ought to go to this wonderful school and become a great man—perhaps at last a chief of our tribe. Mother said that it was good for Indians to be educated, as white men were "so tricky with papers."

I had, up to this time, been leading a very happy life, helping with the planting, trapping, fishing, basket-making and playing all the games of my tribe—which is famous at lacrosse—but the desire to travel and see new things and the hope of finding an easy way to much knowledge in the wonderful school outweighed my regard for my home and its joys, and so I was one of the twelve boys who in 1892 left our reservation to go to the government-contract school for Indians, situated in a large Pennsylvania city and known as the _____ Institute.

Till I arrived at the school I had never heard that there were any other Indians in the country other than those of our reservation, and I did not know that our tribe was called Mohawk. My people called themselves "Ga-nien-ge-ha-ga," meaning "People of the Beacon Stone" and Indians generally they termed "On-give-hon-we," meaning "Real-men" or "Primitive People."

My surprise, therefore, was great when I found myself surrounded in the schoolyard by strange Indian boys belonging to tribes of which I had never heard, and when it was said that my people were only the "civilized Mohawks," I at first thought that "Mohawk" was a nickname and fought any boy who called me by it.

I had left home for the school with a great deal of hope, having said to my mother: "Do not worry. I shall soon return to you a better boy and with a good education!" Little did I dream that that was the last time I would ever see her kind face. She died two years later, and I was not allowed to go to her funeral.

The journey to Philadelphia had been very enjoyable and interesting. It was my first ride on the "great steel horse," as the Indians called the railway train, but my frame of mind changed as soon as my new home was reached.

The first thing that happened to me and to all other freshly caught young redskins when we arrived at the institution was a bath of a particularly disconcerting sort. We were used to baths of the swimming variety, for on the reservation we boys spent a good deal of our time in the water, but this first bath at the institution was different. For one thing, it was accompanied by plenty of soap, and for another thing, it was preceded by a haircut that is better described as a crop.

The little newcomer, thus cropped and delivered over to the untender mercies of larger Indian boys of tribes different from his own, who laughingly attacked his bare skin with very hot water and very hard scrubbing brushes, was likely to emerge from the encounter with a clean skin but perturbed mind. When, in addition, he was prevented from expressing his feelings in the only language he knew, what wonder if some rules of the school were broken.

After the astonishing bath the newcomer was freshly clothed from head to foot, while the raiment in which he came from the reservation was burned or buried. Thereafter he was released by the torturers, and could be seen sidling about the corridors like a lonely crab, silent, sulky, immaculately clean, and most disconsolate.

After my bath and reclothing and after having had my name taken down in the records, I was assigned to a dormitory, and began my regular school life, much to my dissatisfaction. The recording of my name was accompanied by a change which, though it might seem trifling to the teachers, was very important to me. My name among my own people was "Ah-nen-la-de-ni," which in English means "Turning Crowd" or "Turns the Crowd," but my family had had the name "La France" bestowed on them by the French some generations before my birth, and at the institution my Indian name was discarded, and I was informed that I was henceforth to be known as Daniel La France.

It made me feel as if I had lost myself. I had been proud of myself and my possibilities as "Turns the Crowd," for in spite of their civilized surroundings the Indians of our reservation in my time still looked back to the old warlike days when the Mohawks were great people, but Daniel La France was to me a stranger and a nobody with no possibilities. It seemed as if my prospect of a chiefship had vanished. I was very homesick for a long time.

The dormitory to which I was assigned had twenty beds in it and was under a captain, who was one of the advanced scholars. It was his duty to teach and enforce the rules of the place in this room, and to report to the white authorities all breaches of discipline.

Out in the schoolyard there was the same sort of supervision. Whether at work or play, we were constantly watched, and there were those in authority over us. This displeased us Mohawks, who were warriors at fourteen years of age.

After the almost complete freedom of reservation life the cramped quarters and the dull routine of the school were maddening to all us strangers. There were endless rules for us to study and abide by, and hardest of all was the rule against speaking to each other in our own language. We had to speak English or remain silent, and those who knew no English were forced to be dumb or else break the rules in secret. This last we did quite frequently and were punished when detected, by being made to stand in the "public hall" for a long time or to march about the yard while the other boys were at play.

There were about *115* boys at this school, and three miles from us was a similar government school for Indian girls, which had nearly as many inmates.

The system when I first went to this school contemplated every Indian boy learning a trade as well as getting a grammar school education. Accordingly we went to school in the morning and to work in the afternoon, or the other way about.

There were shoemakers, blacksmiths, tinsmiths, farmers, printers, all sorts of mechanics among us. I was set to learn the tailoring trade, and stuck at it for two and a half years, making such progress that I was about to be taught cutting when I began to cough, and it was said that outdoor work would be better for me. Accordingly I went, during the vacation of *1895*, up into Bucks County, Pa., and worked on a farm with benefit to my health, tho people who employed me were quite different from those of our reservation.

After I had finished with the grammar school I got a situation in the office of a lawyer while still residing in the institution. I also took a course of stenography and typewriting at the Philadelphia Young Men's Christian Association. So practically I was only a boarder at the institute during the latter part of my eight years' stay there.

Nevertheless, I was valuable to the authorities there for certain purposes, and when I wanted to leave and go to Carlisle School, which I had heard was very good, I could not obtain permission.

This institute, as I have said, was a government-contract school for teaching Indians. The great exertions made by the agent, who visited our reservation in the first place, were caused by the fact that a certain number of Indian children had to be obtained before the school could be opened. I do not think that the Indian parents signed any papers, but we boys and girls were supposed to remain at the school for five years. After that, as I understand it, we were free from any obligation.

The reason why I and others like me were kept at the school was that we served as show scholars—as results of the system and evidences of the good work the institute was doing.

When I first went to the school the superintendent was a clergyman, honest and well meaning, and during the first five years thereafter while he remained in charge the general administration was honest, but when he went away the school entered upon a period of changing administrations and general demoralization. New superintendents succeeded each other at short intervals, and some of them were violent and cruel, while all seemed to us boys more or less dishonest. Boys who had been inmates of the school for eight years were shown to visitors as results of two years' tuition, and shoes and other articles bought in Philadelphia stores were hung up on the walls at public exhibition or concert and exhibited as the work of us boys. I was good for various show purposes. I could sing and play a musical instrument, and I wrote essays which were thought to be very good. The authorities also were fond of displaying me as one who had come to the school a few years before unable to speak a word of English.

Over the superintendent of the institute there was a Board of Lady Managers with a Lady Directress, and these visited us occasionally, but there was no use laying any complaint before them. They were arbitrary and almost unapproachable. Matters went from bad to worse, and when the Spanish-American War broke out, and my employer, the lawyer, resolved to go to it in the Red Cross service and offered to take me with him I greatly desired to go, but was not allowed. I suppose that the lawyer could easily have obtained my liberty, but did not wish to antagonize the Lady Managers, who considered any criticism of the institution as an attack on their own infallibility.

While waiting for a new situation after the young lawyer had gone away, I heard of the opportunities there were for young men who could become good nurses, and of the place where such training could be secured. I desired to go there and presented this ambition to the superintendent, who at first encouraged me to the extent of giving a fair recommendation. But when the matter was laid before the Head Directress in the shape of an application for admission ready to be sent by me to the authorities of the Nurses' Training School, she flatly refused it consideration without giving any good reason for doing so.

She, however, made the mistake of returning the application to me, and it was amended later and sent to the Training School in Manhattan. It went out through a secret channel, as all the regular mail of the institution's inmates, whether outgoing or incoming, was opened and examined in the office of the superintendent.

A few days before the 4th of July, *1899*, the answer to my application arrived in the form of notice to report at the school for the entrance examination. This communication found me in the school jail, where I had been placed for the first time in all my life at the institution.

I had been charged with throwing a nightgown out of

the dormitory window, and truly it was my nightgown that was found in the schoolyard, for it had my number upon it. But I never threw it out of the window. I believe that one of the official underlings did that in order to found upon it a charge against me, for the school authorities had discovered that I and other boys of the institution had gone to members of the Indian Rights Association and had made complaint of conditions in the school, and that an investigation was coming. They, therefore, desired to disgrace and punish me as one of the leaders of those who were exposing them.

I heard about the letter from the Training School, and was very anxious to get away, but my liberation in time to attend that entrance examination seemed impossible. The days passed, and when the 4th of July arrived I was still in the school jail, which was the rear part of a stable.

At one o'clock my meal of bread and water was brought to me by the guard detailed to look after my safekeeping. After he had delivered this to me he went outside, leaving the door open, but standing there. The only window of that stable was very small, very high on the wall and was protected by iron bars—but here was the door left open.

I fled, and singularly enough the guard had his back turned and was contemplating nature with great assiduity. As soon as I got out of the enclosure I dashed after and caught a trolley car, and a few hours later I was in New York.

That was the last I saw of the institute and it soon afterward went out of existence, but I heard that as a result of the demand for an investigation the Superintendent of Indian Schools had descended on it upon a given day and found everything beautiful—for her visit had been announced. But she returned again the next day, when it was supposed that she had left the city, and then things were not beautiful at all, and much that we had told about was proven.

Elias Garza:
A Mexican American
Family in Conflict

People of Mexican ancestry were absorbed into the United States after a successful war of conquest in the 1840s brought most of the Southwest under American control. Though guaranteed their rights and lands by treaty, they soon found these promises empty. They were deprived of their best lands, denied the vote, and reduced to the status of peasants under white authority. By the beginning of the twentieth century Texas Rangers were directing an attack on Chicanos similar to Ku Klux Klan attacks on African Americans. A reporter for World's Week *wrote: "Some rangers have degenerated into common man-killers. There is no penalty for killing, for no*

jury would ever convict a white man for shooting a Mexican."

Working Mexican Americans had to battle salary differentials that paid far less than whites for the same work. When union organization was attempted and strikes and violence flared in Arizona copper mines and elsewhere, state militia were summoned to suppress union militancy. White judges, schoolteachers, and editors mounted a campaign that undermined economic and cultural independence throughout the Southwest.

Elias Garza, a native of Cuernavaca, found little to enjoy during his long stays in the United States. This is his story as recorded by a social worker.

My life is a real story, especially here in the United States where they drive one crazy from working so much. They squeeze one here until one is left useless, and then one has to go back to Mexico to be a burden to one's countrymen. But the trouble is that is true not only here but over there also. . . .

I began to work when I was twelve years old. My mother was a servant and I worked in one of those old mills which ground sugar cane. I took charge of driving the oxen. They called me the driver. This was on the estate of La Piedad, Michoacán. I think that they paid me $.25 a day and I had to go round and round the mill from the time the sun rose until it set. My mother, as well as I, had to work, because my father died when I was very small.

I went on in that way until when I was fifteen or sixteen I planted corn on my own account on shares. The owners gave us the seed, the animals, and the land, but it turned out that when the crop was harvested there wasn't anything left for us even if we had worked very hard. That was terrible. Those landowners were robbers.

At that time I heard that there were some good jobs here in the United States and that good money could be made. Some other friends accompanied me and we went first to Mexico City and from there we came to Ciudad Juárez. We then went to El Paso and there we took a *renganche* for Kansas. We worked on the tracks, taking up and laying down the rails, removing the old ties and putting in new, and doing all kinds of hard work. They only paid us $1.50 and exploited us without mercy in the commissary camp, for they sold us everything very high. Nevertheless as at that time things generally were cheap I managed to make a little money with which I went back to La Piedad to see my mother. She died a little later and this left me very sad.

I decided to come back to the United States, and I came to Los Angeles, California. Here I married a Mexican young lady. I went to work in a stone quarry. I placed the dynamite and did other work which took some care. They paid me $1.95 a day but I worked ten hours. Later I worked at a railroad station. I worked as a riveter, working a pressure gun for riveting. At that work I earned $1.50 a day for nine hours, but it was very hard. My wife died at that time.

I then got work in a packing plant. I began by earning $1.25 a day there for nine hours of work and I got to earn $4.00 a day for eight hours work. I learned to skin hogs there and slaughter them also. The work was very hard. Later I was married to a woman from San Antonio, Texas.

She was young, beautiful, white, and she had two little children who became my stepchildren. We went to Mexico together. We boarded ship at San Pedro and from there went to Mazatlán until we got to Michoacán. We saw that things were bad there, for that was in *1912*, and the disorders of the revolution had already started; so we came back to the United States by way of Laredo, Texas.

In San Antonio we were under contract to go and pick cotton in a camp in the valley of the Rio Grande. A group of countrymen and my wife and I went to pick. When we arrived at the camp the planter gave us an old hovel which had been used as a chicken house before, to live in, out in the open. I didn't want to live there and told him that if he didn't give us a little house which was a little better we would go. He told us to go, and my wife and I and my children were leaving when the sheriff fell upon us. He took me to the jail and there the planter told them that I wanted to leave without paying him for my passage. He charged me twice the cost of the transportation, and though I tried first not to pay him, and then to pay him what it cost, I couldn't do anything. The authorities would only pay attention to him, and as they were in league with him they told me that if I didn't pay they would take my wife and my little children to work. Then I paid them. From there we went to Dallas, Texas, from where we worked on the tracks as far as El Paso. I kept on at the same work towards Tucson, Arizona, until I got to Los Angeles. I have worked in the packing plants here since then, in cement and other jobs, even as a farm laborer. In spite of it all I have managed to save some money with which I have bought this automobile and some clothes. I have now decided to work in the colony in Mexico and not come back to this country where I have left the best of my youth.

I learned a little English here from hearing it so much. I can read and write it, but I don't even like to deal with those *bolillos* for the truth is that they don't like the Mexicans. Even the *pochos* don't like us. I have scrcely been able to stand up for my rights with the little English that I have learned, but I would like to know a lot of English so as to tell them what they are and in order to defend my poor countrymen. . . .

Once a poor Mexican bought a bottle of whiskey to take to his house to drink it. He had put it in the back pocket of his trousers. That was at night and he was going home. He stopped in front of a workshop to see some goods when he noticed that a policeman was drawing near. Then hc slyly put his hand to his back pocket in order to take the little bottle out and perhaps throw it away when the policeman, without more ado, fired a shot at him and killed him. They didn't do anything to that policeman; he is going about free. And there have been an infinite number of cases like that.

I know of others who at work in the factories have lost an arm of a leg, and they haven't been given a thing. What they do is to take away their jobs. That is why we don't like these people.

I almost am, and almost am not, a Catholic. I remember that when I was very little, over there in Cuernavaca, my mother took me to some exercises of Holy Week and that the priest told all those who were in the church that they should cry for their sins before Christ there in the temple, and they all began to weep and to cry out all that they had done, even my own mother. But I couldn't weep nor did I want to cry out my sins. Since that time I have almost not gone back to the church nor do I pray at home.

I read few newspapers for they almost don't say anything but lies and one comes out from work so tired that one doesn't even want to read papers of any kind. I have almost never read books; once in a long time I do read books of stories of Mexicans.

I have always tried to be close to my countrymen and defend them, but there are some who are neither united nor do they want to defend themselves; that is why the Americans look down on us as they do.

Antanas Kaztaukis:
From Lithuania
to Chicago's Stockyards

By 1893, when a mammoth Chicago fair celebrated the four hundredth anniversary of Columbus's arrival in America, that city had become a typical American metropolis. The population had grown from less than 30,000 in 1851 to over a million at the time of the Columbian Exposition. The vast majority of its inhabitants—seven out of ten—were foreign born. Most lived in crowded slums and worked hard at low-paying jobs. The city's 165 square miles roared with industrial activity. Noisy railroads, factory machinery, and pungent smells from the stockyards gave the city a unique character.

217

Among the thousands from abroad who poured into the city to find work was one who wrote the short memoir that follows. He used the pseudonym Antanas Kaztaukis because he feared the Russian government would punish his father and friend in Lithuania should he sign his real name.

A few years after the appearance of Antana's story, Upton Sinclair published The Jungle, *an explosive exposé of immigrant labor exploitation in the meat-packing industry of Chicago. Based on nine months Sinclair spent with a European family recently arrived in the United States,* The Jungle *brought congressional passage of a Pure Food and Drug Act and sparked a greater interest in socialism.*

Antanas Kaztaukis offered no such answer in his biography, but drew hope and inspiration from his ability to survive and from the purpose and comradeship he found in the trade union movement.

It was the shoemaker who made me want to come to America. He was a traveling shoemaker, for on our farms we tan our own cowhides, and the shoemaker came to make them into boots for us. By traveling he learned all the news and he smuggled in newspapers across the frontier from Germany. We were always glad to hear him talk.

I can never forget that evening four years ago. It was a cold December. We were in a big room in our log house in Lithuania. My good, kind, thin old mother sat near the wide fireplace, working her brown spinning wheel, with which she made cloth for our skirts and coats and pants. I sat on the floor in front of her with my knee-boots off and my feet stretched out to the fire. My father sat and smoked his pipe across the fireplace. Between was a kerosene lamp on a table, and under it sat the ugly shoemaker on a stool finishing a big yellow boot. I kept watching him. My fat, older brother, who sat behind with his fat wife, grinned and said: "Look out or your eyes will makes holes in the leather." My brother's eyes were always dull and sleepy. Men like him stay in Lithuania.

At last the boot was finished. The little shoemaker held it up and looked at it.

"That's a good boot," said my father.

The shoemaker grunted. "That's a damn poor boot," he replied (instead of "damn" he said "skatina"), "a rough boot like all your boots, and so when you grow old you are lame. You have only poor things, for rich Russians get your good things, and yet you will not kick up against them. Bah!"

"I don't like your talk," said my father, and he spit into the fire, as he always did when he began to think. "I am honest. I work hard. We get along. That's all. So what good will such talk do me?"

"You!" cried the shoemaker, and he now threw the boot on the floor so that our big dog lifted up his head and looked around. "It's not you at all. It's the boy—that boy there!" and he pointed to me. "That boy must go to America!"

My mother looked frightened and she put her hand on my head. "No, no; he is only a boy," she said.

"Bah!" cried the shoemaker. "He is eighteen and a man. You know where he must go in three years more."

We all knew he meant my five years in the army.

"Where is your oldest son? Dead. Oh, I know the Russians, they let him soak in rain, standing guard all night in the snow and ice he froze, the food was God's food, the vodka was cheap and rotten! Then he died."

He pulled out an old American newspaper, printed in the Lithuanian language, and I remembered he tore it he was so angry. "The world's good news is all kept away. We can only read what Russian officials print in their papers. Read? No, you can't read or write your own language, because there is no Lithuanian school—only the Russian school—[and] even those Russian schools make you pay to learn, and you have no money to pay. Will you never be ashamed—all you? Listen to me."

My fat brother grinned and said to the shoemaker, "You always stir up young men to go to America. Why don't you go yourself?"

"I am too old," he said, "to learn a new trade. These boots are no good in America. America is no place for us old rascals. My son is in Chicago in the stockyards, and he writes to me. They have hard knocks. If you are sick or old there and have no money you must die. That Chicago place has trouble, too. Do you see the light? That is kerosene. Do you remember the price went up last year? That is Rockefeller. My son writes me about him. He is another man wolf. A few men like him are grabbing all the good things—the oil and coal and meat and everything. But against these men you can strike if you are young. You can read free papers and prayer books. You can have free meetings and talk out what you think. And so if you are young you can change all these troubles. But I am old. I can feel it now, this winter. So I only tell young men to go." He looked hard at me and I looked at him.

He kept looking at me, but he opened the newspaper and held it up. "Someday," he said, "I will be caught and sent to jail, but I don't care. I got this from my son, who reads all he can find at night. It had to be smuggled in. I lend it many times to many young men. My son got it from the night school and he put it in Lithuanian for me to see." Then he bent over the paper a long time and his lips moved. At last he looked into the fire and fixed his hair, and then his voice was shaking and very low: "We know these are true things—that all men are born free and equal—that God gives them rights which no man can take away—that among these rights are life, liberty, and the getting of happiness."

He stopped, I remember, and looked at me, and I was not breathing. He said it again. "'Life, liberty, and the getting of happiness.' Oh, that is what you want."

My mother began to cry. "He cannot go if his father commands him to stay," she kept saying. I knew this was true, for in Lithuania a father can command his son till he dies.

"No, he must not go," said the shoemaker, "if his father commands him to stay." He turned and looked hard at my father. My father was looking into the fire. In about five minutes the shoemaker got up and asked, "Well, what do you say—the army or America?" But my father shook his head and would not say anything.

After he was gone my father and I kept looking at the fire. My old mother stopped spinning and put her hand on my forehead.

"Alexandria is a fine girl," she whispered. This gave me a quick bad feeling. Alexandria was the girl I wanted to marry. She lived about ten miles away. Her father liked my father and they seemed to be glad that I loved her. My old mother kept her hands moving on my forehead. "Yes, she is a nice girl; a kind, beautiful girl," she kept whispering. We sat there till the lamp went out. Then the fire got low and the room was cold and we went to bed. But I could not sleep and kept thinking.

The next day my father told me that I could not go until the time came for the army, three years ahead. "Stay until then and then we will see," he said. My mother was very glad and so was I, because of Alexandria. But in the coldest part of that winter my dear old mother got sick and died.

That summer the shoemaker came again and talked with me. This time I was very eager to go to America, and my father told me I could go.

One morning I walked over to say good-by to Alexandria. When I saw her I felt very bad, and so did she. I had the strongest wish I ever had to take hold of her and keep her all my life. We stayed together till it was dark and night fogs came up out of the field grass, and we could hardly see the house. Then she said good-by. For many nights I kept remembering the way she looked up at me.

The next night after supper I started. It is against the law to sell tickets to America, but my father saw the secret agent in the village and he got a ticket from Germany and found us a guide. I had bread and cheese and honey and vodka and clothes in my bag. Some of the neighbors walked a few miles and said good-by and then went back. My father and my younger brother walked on all night with the guide and me. At daylight we came to the house of a man the guide knew. We slept there and that night I left my father and young brother. My father gave me $50 besides my ticket. The next morning before light we were going through the woods and we came to the frontier. Three roads run along the frontier. On the first road there is a soldier every mile, who stands there all night. On the second road is a soldier every half mile, and on the third road is a soldier every quarter of a mile. This guide went ahead through the woods. I hid with my big bag behind a bush and whenever he raised his hand I sneaked along. I felt cold all over and sometimes hot. He told me that sometimes he took twenty immigrants together, all without passports, and then he could not pass the soldiers and so he paid a soldier he knew one dollar a head to let them by. He said the soldier was very strict and counted them to see that he was not being cheated.

So I was in Germany. Two days after that we reached Tilzit and the guide took me to the railroad man. This man had a crowd of immigrants in a room, and we started that night on the railroad—fourth class. It was bad riding sometimes. I used to think of Alexandria. We were all green and slow. The railroad man used to say to me, "You will have to be quicker than this in Chicago," and he was right. We were very slow in the stations where we changed trains, and he used to shout at us then, and one old German man who spoke Lithuanian told me what the man was calling us. When he told me this I hurried, and so did the others, and we began to learn to be quicker. It took three days to get to Hamburg. There we were put in a big house called a barracks, and we waited a week. The old German man told me that the barracks men were cheating us. He had been once to Cincinnati in America to visit his son, who kept a saloon. His old, long pipe was stolen there. He kept saying, "Dem grafters, dem grafters," in a low voice whenever they brought food to sell, for our bags were now empty. They kept us there till our money was half spent on food. I asked the old man what kind of American men were grafters, and he said, "

All kinds in Cincinnati, but more in Chicago!" I knew I was going to Chicago, and I began to think quicker. I thought quicker yet on the boat. I saw men playing cards. I played and lost $1.86 in my new money, till the old man came behind me and said, "Dem grafters." When I heard this I got scared and threw down my cards. That old man used to point up at the rich people looking down at us and say "Dem grafters." They were the richest people I had ever seen—the boat was the biggest boat I had ever seen—the machine that made it go was very big, and so was the horn that blew in a fog. I felt everything get bigger and go quicker every day.

It was the most when we came to New York. We were driven in a thick crowd to the railroad station. Everything got quicker—worse and worse—till then at last I was in a boarding house by the stockyards in Chicago, with three Lithuanians who knew my father's sisters at home.

That first night we sat around in the house and they asked me, "Well, why did you come?" I told them about that first night and what the ugly shoemaker said about "life, liberty, and the getting of happiness." They all leaned back and laughed. "What you need is money," they said.

"It was all right at home. You wanted nothing. You ate your own meat and your own things on the farm. You made your own clothes and had your own leather. The other things you got at the Jew man's store and paid him with sacks of rye. But here you want a hundred things. Whenever you walk out you see new things you want, and you must have money to buy everything."

Then one man asked me, "How much have you?" and I told him $30. "You must buy clothes to look rich, even if you are not rich," he said. "With good clothes you will have friends."

The next morning three of these men took me to a store near the stockyards to buy a coat and pants. "Look out," said one of them. "Is he a grafter?" I asked. They all laughed. "You stand still. That is all you have to do," they said. So the Jew man kept putting on coats and I moved my arms and back and sides when they told me. We stayed there till it was time for dinner. Then we bought a suit. I paid $5 and then I was to pay $1 a week for five weeks.

In the afternoon I went to a big store. There was a man named Elias. "He is not a grafter," said my friends. He was nice to me and gave me good advice how to get a job. I bought two shirts, a hat, a collar, a necktie, two pairs of socks, and some shoes. We kept going upstairs and downstairs. I saw one Lithuanian man buying everything for his wife and three children, who would come here the next week from Lithuania. My things cost me $8. I put these on right away and then I began to feel better.

The next night they took me for a walk downtown. We would not pay to ride, so we walked so long that I wanted to take my shoes off, but I did not tell them this. When we came there I forgot my feet. We stood by one theater and watched for half an hour. Then we walked all around a store that filled one whole block and had walls of glass. Then we had a drink of whisky, and this is better than vodka. We felt happier and looked into *cafés*. We saw shiny carriages and automobiles. I saw men with dress suits, I saw women with such clothes that I could not think at all. Then my friends punched me and I turned around and saw one of these women, and with her was a gentleman in a fine dress suit. "He is a grafter," said my friends. "See what money can do." Then we walked home and I felt poor and my shoes got very bad.

That night I felt worse. We were tired out when we reached the stockyards, so we stopped on the bridge and looked into the river out there. It was so full of grease and dirt and sticks and boxes that it looked like a big, wide, dirty street, except in some places, where it boiled up. It made me sick to look at it. When I looked away I could see on one side some big fields full of holes, and these were the city dumps. On the other side were the stockyards, with twenty tall slaughter-house chimneys. The wind blew a big smell from them to us. Then we walked on between the yards and the dumps and all the houses looked bad and poor. In our house my room was in the basement. I lay down on the floor with three other men and the air was rotten. I did not go to sleep for a long time. I knew then that money was everything I needed. My money was almost gone and I thought that I would soon die unless I got a job, for this was not like home. Here money was everything and a man without money must die.

The next morning my friends woke me up at five o'clock and said, "Now, if you want life, liberty, and happiness," they laughed, "you must push for yourself. You must get a job. Come with us." And we went to the yards. Men and women were walking in by thousands as far as we could see. We went to the doors of one big slaughter house. There was a crowd of about *200* men waiting there for a job. They looked hungry and kept watching the door. At last a special policeman came out and began pointing to men, one by one. Each one jumped forward. Twenty-three were taken. Then they all went inside, and all the others turned their faces away and looked tired. I remember one boy sat down and cried, just next to me, on a pile of boards. Some policemen waved their clubs and we all walked on. I found some Lithuanians to talk with, who told me they had come every morning for three weeks. Soon we met other crowds coming away from other slaughter houses, and we all walked around and felt bad and tired and hungry.

That night I told my friends that I would not do this many days, but would go someplace else. "Where?" they asked me, and I began to see then that I was in bad trouble, because I spoke no English. Then one man told me to give him $5 to give the special policeman. I did this and the next morning the policeman pointed me out, so I had a job. I have heard some big talk since then about my American freedom of contract, but I do not think I had much freedom in bargaining for this job with the Meat Trust. My job was in the cattle killing room. I pushed the blood along the gutter. Some people think these jobs make men bad. I do not think so. The men who do the killing are not as bad as the ladies with fine clothes who come every day to look at it, because they have to do it. The cattle do not suffer. They are knocked senseless with a big hammer and are dead before they wake up. This is done not to spare them pain, but because if they got hot and sweating with fear and pain the meat would not be so good. I soon saw that every job in the room was done like this—so as to save everything and make money. One Lithuanian who worked with me said, "They get all the blood out of those cattle and all the work out of us men." This was true, for we worked that first day from six in the morning till seven at night. The next day we worked from six in the morning till eight at night. The next day we had no work. So we had no good, regular hours. It was hot in the room that summer, and the hot blood made it worse.

I held this job six weeks and then I was turned off. I think some other man had paid for my job, or perhaps I was too slow. The foreman in that room wanted quick men to make the work rush, because he was paid more if the work was done cheaper and quicker. I saw now that every man was helping himself, always trying to get all the money he could. At that time I believed that all men in Chicago were grafters when they had to be. They only wanted to push themselves. Now, when I was idle I began to look about, and everywhere I saw sharp men beating out slow men like me. Even if we worked hard it did us no good. I had saved $13— $5 a week for six weeks makes $30, and take off $15 for six weeks' board and lodging and $2 for the other things. I showed this to a Lithuanian who had been here two years, and he laughed. "It will be taken from you," he said. He had saved a hundred dollars once and had begun to buy a house on the installment plan, but something had happened that he did not know about and his landlord put him out and kept the hundred dollars. I found that many Lithuanians had been beaten this way. At home we never made a man sign contract papers. We only had him make the sign of a cross and promise he would do what he said. But this was no good in Chicago. So these sharp men were beating us.

I saw this, too, in the newspaper. I was beginning to learn English, and at night in the boarding house the men who did not play cards used to read the paper to us. The biggest word was "graft" in red letters on the front page. Another word was "trust." This paper kept putting these two words together. Then I began to see how every American man was trying to get money for himself. I wondered if the old German man in Cincinnati had found his pipe yet. I felt very bad and sorrowful in that month. I kept walking around with many other Lithuanians who had no job. Our money was going and we could find nothing to do. At night we got homesick for our fine green mountains. We read all the news about home in our Lithuanian Chicago newspaper, *The Katalikas*. It is a good paper and gives all the news. In the same office we bought this song, which was written in Brooklyn by P. Brandukas. He, too, was homesick. It is sung all over Chicago now and you can hear it in the summer evenings through the open windows. In English it is something like this:

Oh, Lithuania, so dear to me,
Good-by to you, my Fatherland.
Sorrowful in my heart I leave you,
I know not who will stay to guard you.

Is it enough for me to live and enjoy between
  my neighbors,
In the woods with the flowers and birds?
Is it enough for me to live peaceful between
  my friends?
No, I must go away form my old father and mother.

The sun shines bright,
The flowers smell sweet.
The birds are singing,
They make the country glad;
But I cannot sing because I must leave you.

Those were bad days and nights. At last I had a chance to help myself. Summer was over and Election Day was coming. The Republican boss in our district, Jonidas, was a saloonkeeper. A friend took me there. Jonidas shook hands and treated me fine. He taught me to sign my name, and the next week I went with him to an office and signed some paper, and then I could vote. I voted as I was told, and then they got me back into the yards to work, because one big politician owns stock in one of those houses. Then I felt that I was getting in beside the game. I was in a combine like other sharp men. Even when work was slack I was all right, because they got me a job in the street-cleaning department. I felt proud, and I went to the back room in Jonida's saloon and got him to write a letter to Alexandria to tell her she must come soon and be my wife.

But this was just the trouble. All of us were telling our friends to come soon. Soon they came—even thousands. The employers in the yard liked this, because those sharp foremen are inventing new machines and the work is easier to learn, and so these slow Lithuanians and even green girls can learn to do it, and then the Americans and Germans and Irish are put out and the employer saves money, because the Lithuanians work cheaper. This was why the American labor unions began to organize us all just the same as they had organized the Bohemians and Poles before us.

Well, we were glad to be organized. We had learned that in Chicago every man must push himself always, and Jonidas had taught us how much better we could push ourselves by getting into a combine. Now, we saw that this union was the best combine for us, because it was the only combine that could say, "It is our business to raise your wages."

But that Jonidas—he spoiled our first union. He was sharp. First he got us to hire the room over his saloon. He used to come in at our meetings and sit in the back seat and grin. There was an Irishman there from the union headquarters, and he was trying to teach us to run ourselves. He talked to a Lithuanian, and the Lithuanian said it to us, but we were slow to do things, and we were jealous and were always jumping up to shout and fight. So the Irishman used to wipe his hot red face and call us bad names. He told the Lithuanian not to say these names to us, but Jonidas heard them, and in his saloon, where we all went down after the meeting when the Irishman was gone, Jonidas gave us free drinks and then told us the names. I will not write them here.

One night that Irishman did not come and Jonidas saw his chance and took the chair. He talked very fine and we elected him president. We made him treasurer, too. Down in the saloon he gave us free drinks and told us we must break away from the Irish grafters. The next week he made us strike, all by himself. We met twice a day in the saloon and spent all of our money on drinks and then the strike was over. I got out of this union after that. I had been working hard in the cattle killing room and I had a better job. I was called a cattle butcher now and I joined the Cattle Butchers' Union. This union is honest and it has done me a great deal of good.

It has raised my wages. The man who worked at my job before the union came was getting through the year an average of $9 a week. I am getting $11. In my first job I got $5 a week. The man who works there now gets $5.75.

It has given me more time to learn to read and speak and enjoy life like an American. I never work now from 6 a.m. to 9 p.m. and then be idle the next day. I work now from 7 a.m. to 5:30 p.m., and there are not so many idle days. The work is evened up.

With more time and more money I live much better and I am very happy. So is Alexandria. She came a year ago and has learned to speak English already. Some of the women go to the big store the day they get here, when they have not even sense to pick out the clothes that look right, but Alexandria waited three weeks till she knew, and so now she looks the finest of any woman in the district. We have four nice rooms, which she keeps very clean, and she has flowers growing in boxes in the two front windows. We do not go much to church, because the church seems to be too slow. But we belong to a Lithuanian society that gives two picnics in summer and two big balls in winter, where we have a fine time. I go one night a week to the Lithuanian Concertina Club. On Sundays we go on the trolley out into the country.

But we like to stay at home more now because we have a baby. When he grows up I will not send him to the Lithuanian Catholic school. They have only two bad rooms and two priests, who teach only in Lithuanian from prayer books. I will send him to the American school, which is very big and good. The teachers there are Americans and they belong to the Teachers' Labor Union, which has three thousand teachers and belongs to our Chicago Federation of Labor. I am sure that such teachers will give him a good chance.

Our union sent a committee to Springfield last year and they passed a law which prevents boys and girls below sixteen from working in the stockyards.

We are trying to make the employers pay on Saturday night in cash. Now they pay in checks and the men have to get money the same night to buy things for Sunday, and the saloons cash checks by thousands. You have to take one drink to have the check cashed. It is hard to take one drink.

The union is doing another good thing. It is combining all the nationalities. The night I joined the Cattle Butchers' Union I was led into the room by a Negro member. With me were Bohemians, Germans, and Poles, and Mike Donnelly, the president, is an Irishman. He spoke to us in English and then three interpreters told us what he said. We swore to be loyal to our union above everything else except the country, the city and the state—to be faithful to each other—to protect the women workers—to do our best to understand the history of the labor movement, and to do all we could to help it on. Since then I have gone there every two weeks and I help the movement, by being an interpreter for the other Lithuanians who come in. That is why I have learned to speak and write good English. The others do not need me long. They soon learn English, too, and when they have done that they are quickly becoming Americans.

But the best thing the union does is to make me feel more independent. I do not have to pay to get a job and I cannot be discharged unless I am no good. For almost the whole *30,000* men and women are organized now in some one of our unions and they all are directed by our central council. No man knows what it means to be sure of his job unless he been fired like I was once without any reason being given.

So this is why I joined the labor union. There are many better stories than mine, for my story is very common. There are thousands of immigrants like me. Over *300,000* immigrants have been organized in the last three years by the American Federation of Labor. The immigrants are glad to be organized if the leaders are as honest as Mike Donnelly is. You must get money to live well and to get money you must combine. I cannot bargain alone with the Meat Trust. I tried it and it does not work.

My young brother came over three weeks ago, to escape being sent out to fight in Japan. I tried to have my father come, too, but he was too old. I wish that ugly little shoemaker would come. He would make a good walking delegate.

A Collar Starcher

Although women were five million strong in the labor force by 1900, trade unions shunned them almost as much as they did racial and ethnic minorities. Women's permanent place was in the home, it was said, and their loyalty to jobs and unions could only be temporary. Women often felt little personal investment in their jobs, unions, or strikes, except when other alternatives failed. Women were told it was unladylike to join a union, particularly since unions were run by "labor agitators" and foreigners committed to socialism or anarchism. Just as men believed in the American dream and hoped that hard work or ingenious invention would release them from grueling labor, most women dreamed that marriage and

motherhood would do the same for them.

But as the nineteenth century gave way to the twentieth, the unreality of such dreams became more evident. Disillusioned, women joined unions and struck for higher wages, better working conditions, and union recognition. They began to play a key part in labor disputes, providing the industrial scene with some of its most vivid moments. Fearing her recent part in a laundry workers' strike in Troy, New York, would result in her being blacklisted in the industry, this collar starcher dictated her memoir to a sympathetic female reporter but she stipulated that her name be withheld.

When I left school at the age of sixteen to go to work there were very few opportunities open to young girls, for the time was nearly thirty years ago. Therefore I considered myself unusually lucky to have been born and brought up in Troy, New York, where the shirt and collar factories offered employment to women. I was lucky also in being a large, stout girl, for the work offered me when I applied was that of a collar starcher, and while this does not call for much muscle, it certainly requires endurance and a good constitution. In those days practically all the laundry work was done by hand. There were no ironing machines and very few washing machines. The starching was about all there was for a girl of sixteen. So a starcher I became and a starcher I am to this day, or rather, I was until the strike came in May.

I thoroughly enjoyed my first working years. The factory was not at all a bad place. I worked side by side with my friends, the girls I had gone to school with, met at church and at dances and picnics. The starching rooms were very hot and stuffy generally, like a Turkish bath, and the work was hard on the hands; but I didn't mind these discomforts. Looking back at it now I think we were very well off. There was nothing like the rush and hurry we live in now. We were not driven at such a furious pace, for, of course, there was not nearly the business done then that there is now.

The starching itself was a very different affair. The collars were two-ply, instead of the thick, unwieldy things men wear now, and there was no "lady work," as we say. We simply rubbed in heavy starch, using our hands and soft cloths. It was hot enough, but not the scalding work it is now.

The working hours were not too long—about eight hours a day. We went to work at nine o'clock, except in the busy season, when we were on hand at eight. The day passed quickly with the talk and sometimes a bit of song to liven things up. We used to sing part-songs and old-fashioned choruses. Some of the girls had beautiful voices.

We have to be at the tables at seven now and an ambitious worker is usually in the factory half an hour before the whistle blows, to get her table ready. As for talk or singing, the foreman would have a fit if anything like that should happen. In our factory all talking is strictly forbidden. You run the risk of instant dismissal if you even speak to the girl across the table. Even at the noon hour you can only whisper. I've seen girls discharged for talking and I know of a case where a girl lost her job for sneezing. The foreman said she did it on purpose. They are not as hard as this in all the factories. Much depends on the foreman.

My father and mother died before I was twenty. We had

our little home and my brother and my three sisters and I lived on there. Three of us girls worked in the factories and one sister stayed at home and kept house for us. Our combined wages made a pretty good income. We lived well, dressed well, and were very happy. My brother married and went West to live. The housekeeping sister married next and then my youngest sister found a husband. That broke up the home, for the two that were left couldn't afford to keep it up. We took a couple of rooms and did our little housekeeping early in the morning before we went to work.

At this time there came a break in the monotony of my life. I married a young man I had known for a number of years. He was an iron molder and made good wages. We went to housekeeping and I thought my collar starching days were over forever. But my husband was taken ill, and before I realized that he was seriously sick I was a widow with a two-year-old daughter to support.

I naturally thought of the factory, but a friend who kept a grocery store begged me to come to live with her and help her with the business. I stayed at the store for eighteen months and at the end of that time I married again, a young telegraph operator I met in the store.

You see I have really done my best to fulfill what the ministers and others often tell us is the true destiny of a woman—to be a wife and mother. But the fates have been against me. My second husband had incipient consumption when I married him, although neither of us knew it. He died after a short illness and six months later my little boy was born. Before the baby was a month old I was back in the factory, a starcher girl once more. Except for this interval of six years I have earned my living starching collars at four cents the dozen.

A Collar Starcher

I have managed to bring up my two children fairly well. They have gone to school and my daughter has had music and dancing lessons. She is thirteen now and beginning to think of learning a trade. I shall not allow her to become a starcher. My boy is ten. He is very fond of his books and I shall try to put him through the high school. I don't know exactly how it is to be done, especially if the Employers' Association succeeds in cutting our wages in half.

There are many married women and widows in the factories in Troy. Of the married women, some have been deserted and others have gone to work because their husbands could not seem to make a living. It seems to me that in a community where the women greatly outnumber the men, the men get discouraged and deteriorate. Very few of the girls in Troy look forward with enthusiasm to marriage. If they are making fairly good wages they hesitate before giving up their jobs. They have too many object lessons around them of women who have come back to the factories after a few years of married life, all their gaiety and high spirits gone and two or three children at home to support. It is a mystery to me how they bring up their children so well. I had friends to help me with mine and I suppose the others have. It means sitting up until all hours sewing, mending, and washing little clothes. After all, a working mother is like any other woman; she wants her children to wear pretty dresses and starched white petticoats.

Collar starching cannot be classed with unskilled labor. It requires considerable intelligence and a knack of handling the starch so as to get it smoothly through the goods. The starchers work very quickly, of course. They have to, both for the sake of the collars and for the sake of their wages. It is possible to starch fifty dozen or more a day, depending on the style of collar. I have often done so. If the work kept up at such a pace a starcher's wages would amount to ten or twelve dollars a week, but, unfortunately, the busy season lasts only three months in the year. A good starcher makes as high as fifteen or sixteen dollars a week during those three months. The rest of the year she is lucky if she makes seven dollars a week. The average, I think, is about six. The average wage the year round is between eight and nine dollars.

In order to make good money during the busy season I get up at half-past five in the morning, prepare a hasty breakfast, leaving the dishes for my daughter to wash. By half-past six I am at work. In the middle of the morning I stop just long enough to take a cup of coffee and a piece of bread, which stay me until lunchtime. Ten minutes' pause for lunch and I am hard at work again. Sometimes I work as late as eight o'clock. When I get home my daughter has my dinner ready for me. A year or two ago I used to have to get it myself after the work was over. Then, often there was washing to be done, for I am obliged in my factory to wear a white gown. Dark calico doesn't present such an attractive appearance, you know.

Many women have it harder than I. One friend of mine has two children and a bedridden mother to care for after hours, and just before the strike her husband was brought home with a broken hip.

I have said that a girl in our factory could make between eight and nine dollars a week the year round. The books will show that this is true, but the fact is you can't find out all there is to factory work by looking at the books. You can't find out, for instance, how much of the employees' wages go back to the firm in the shape of fines. To be docked two dollars a week is the commonest thing in the world at our factory. We expect it, in fact, and are thankful when its amounts to no more.

When I go to work in the morning I am given a slip of paper marked on one side "Received" and on the other "Returned." I mark on the one side the number of collars I receive. When the collars are starched I turn them over to boys from sixteen to twenty and they are sent to the drying rods. These boys mark on the other side of the slip the number of collars returned. If a boy makes a miscount or if for any reason at all the numbers do not tally on both sides of the slip, the starcher is docked. The amount docked from her wages is purely arbitrary. If she is short a dozen of work she is charged from fifty cents to a dollar. If the return side contains a dozen more collars than the starcher appears to have received the starcher is docked ten cents and is not paid for the work she is credited with doing. The great majority of the girls are docked every week in this matter of the received and returned slip. The boys are never docked, it being assumed, apparently, that they never make mistakes. But we no longer even wonder why these unjust distinctions are made.

If a starcher drops one collar on the floor she is docked five dozen collars. In other words for every collar dropped on the floor the girl must starch five dozen collars for nothing. The starcher is even held responsible after the collars leave her hands. If the bars on which the collars are dried happen to be dirty, the starcher is fined, although the bars are supposed to be cleaned by other workers. If a collar drops from the cleaning bars and is found on the floor, the four girls whose work is nearest are fined. Since it is not possible accurately to locate the careless one the four are punished in order to fine the right one.

These are not all the excuses for docking, but they are the most flagrant and unjust ones. It has been said on good authority that our firm alone has recovered from its employees, in fines, $159,900, during the past ten years.

Our position seemed pretty hopeless last August, just a year ago, when our present troubles began. At that time several firms in the association put in starching machines. We had no objection to machines, nor have we now, provided the machines do the work. We would welcome any device which made our task easier or enabled us to turn out more work. I want to make that point clear at the outset.

The machines were brought in but the table starchers were not put to work on them at once. Young girls were brought in from the outside and were set to work in a room by themselves. These girls until just before the strike were not subjected to the same conditions that the table starchers were under. They were given only the easiest work; they were allowed helpers, so that they never had to leave their tables. In this way they were able to make very fair wages, the payroll, in fact, showing they received about the same as the table starchers, who were receiving larger pay per dozen collars. Then the table starchers were informed that hereafter all starching would be done by machinery and that wages would be cut to two cents a dozen. At the same time they began to lay off ten girls a week.

The great majority of the girls were entirely ignorant of labor union methods. Most of us had never even read any labor literature. But every one of us realized that the time had come when we must organize. The first thing the union did was to agree, instead of having these girls laid off, to share our work with them. We were anxious to retain the girls for more reasons than one. For instance, we were puzzled to understand why they were laid off. We knew that there was no shortage of work, for the firms were actually sending work out to other shops.

We next agreed to try the machines, and we maintain that we did give them a fair trial. They were put in some time in August, and the strike did not come until the 4th of May following. We experimented with them long enough to convince all the starchers, including the new ones who had never starched after the tables, that the machines did not and could not starch the collars. The starchers were supposed to only have to rub the work over lightly after it left the machines, but the fact is they had to do as much to the collars after they came out of the machine as they did to the hand-starched work. The machine work resulted in stiff welts in the loose linings of the collars, and these welts we had to beat and soak out, and often restarch the whole collar, making the process longer and harder than it had ever been, with a cut of fifty percent in our wages.

Why should the firms have put in such machines? We asked ourselves the question, and at first it seemed like another of the experiments they try from time to time, experiments which the workers are made to pay for. One such experiment was the use of a certain kind of starch, presumable a cheaper quality than had been used, for the end and aim of all manufacturers is, of course, to lower the cost of production. I shall never forget that starch. It was a German importation. We tried very hard to use it, knowing, of course, that we would be docked if the work was unsatisfactory. It was impossible for us to get it into the linen, and our work all came out soft. We were docked, tried the starch again and were again docked. Then we struck, but our union was too weak to hold out. We went back, tried the starch three days more with the same result and finally convinced the firm that the starch was no good. We paid for that experiment with something like a week's wages.

Knowing the uselessness of combating an experiment we kept on at the machines for a little while after we saw that they could not do the work. The factory was all upside down. One day one thing would be said and the next day another. Three cents a dozen for hand work began to be talked about, and then, all of a sudden, the light broke upon us. The whole thing was clear. The machines were merely a subterfuge to reduce wages.

The table starchers and the machine starchers held a meeting and discussed the situation. We agreed that we could not stand a reduction of fifty percent. We felt that we could have to grant something to save ourselves, so we agreed to accept a reduction of twenty-five percent by working after the machines, with bunchers and hangers up, but we were firm in our determination to stand by our old wages for table work. Meanwhile small groups of girls were being discharged and laid off.

We appointed a committee to call on the head of the firm. He refused to let the committee into his office. Twice was the committee refused an interview. Then we struck. The girls remained in the workrooms until one of the firm came in. He said that he had business at the armory and could not talk to them. The leader asked when he would be willing to discuss matters. He said: "You must first go back to work, and I will consider about giving you a hearing at some future date."

The girls refused to go back to work until the matter of discharging and the matter of wages were discussed, and that night they were all discharged.

Several attempts were made to patch up the trouble. The Commissioner of Labor tried to intervene and the State Board of Mediation, I think it is called, did what it could. The Chamber of Commerce also tried. Arbitration was all the girls asked for, but they insisted that the arbitration come before they went back to work. President Shea of the Federation of Labor and George Waldron, a delegate of the federation, were chosen to confer with our firm. The firm referred them to the Manufacturers' Association. The association refused to meet the men but agreed to meet a committee of the starchers. On May 11 the starchers met the association, and two days later they met them again. Nothing came of either meeting, and a few days later all the girls walked out, not only from our factory, but from the nine in the association. The immediate cause of the sympathetic strike was the action of the other factories in taking the laundry work of the factory where the strike occurred. We have been much blamed for this sympathetic strike. As for me, I cannot see the difference between our sympathetic strike and the sympathetic action of the factories in the association.

We have been out ever since. At first there were small riots. We picketed the factories and tried by all peaceable means to prevent the non-union girls hired to take our places from entering. Some of them turned back ashamed, but others persisted in going in. These girls had their hair pulled and their faces slapped. I am not concealing that. The non-union girls were certainly terrorized. A few of them were handled pretty roughly. We have been denounced for this. Well, there may be better methods of preventing thoughtless and heartless girls from injuring their class, and thereby injuring themselves. I wish I knew what they were. Many of these girls were not in the permanent working class. They became strikebreakers from ignorance and want of reflection, most of them. Others probably belonged to the class that out of pure snobbery opposes organization. They will not join a union because they do not wish to officially ally themselves with the working classes.

We have allied ourselves with the national body of the Laundry Workers' Union and receive strike benefits from them. Some of the girls whose sisters are working, voluntarily do without the benefit money; so there is enough to support the others. Some have left Troy and have found work in other towns. The rest of us are still doing picket duty and are holding the union together in all ways we know of. We have every confidence in our leaders.

The sympathy we have met with in the town has been very encouraging. One merchant gave us $500 cash and another gives us $25 a week. Of course most of the merchants are afraid to offend the manufacturers, whose patronage is worth more than that of the workers. The churches generally are thoroughly down on the strikers and our own ministers tell us that we ought to submit ourselves to the terms our kind employers are good enough to offer us. The head of my firm is one of the most generous contributors to the Y.M.C.A. and has helped build and renovate two churches. He is called an active Christian and is very much looked up to by the best people in Troy. Others in the Employers' Association are splendid churchmen. The Sunday schools and the church societies have a great hold on many of the stitchers and banders. For this reason large numbers of them hold out against a sympathetic strike of the operatives. They tell us privately that they hope we will win and if we do they will probably form unions of their own. That is always the way and we do not complain.

Meanwhile there is one comforting feature: the Employers' Association, in order to save money, is spending it. They have to send all their laundry work out of town to get it done. Some of it goes as far away as Chicago. Their express bills must be something awful.

There is one more little bit of comfort. You ought to see how fat and rosy the girls are getting in the open air. Girls who didn't look like anything are as pretty as pinks since they began to do picket duty.

Becoming a Policeman

By the end of the nineteenth century, many moralists, ministers, and reformers had denounced U.S. cities as ungovernable dens of vice, corruption, and lawlessness. Charged with keeping this bubbling cauldron from boiling over was the lowly cop on the beat. Armed with a billy club, a pistol, and an inadequate knowledge and appreciation of civil liberties and justice, he was asked to bring public behavior into line with society's professed moral standards. He was hamstrung by a top command who took orders from the political and business forces that benefited from crime.

Police departments did not select recruits with any regard for moral qualities. In fact, recruits were usually obliged to use bribes and politics to join the force. Since police work was dangerous and not particularly well paid, recruits generally came from the poor and were overawed by those with power or money.

In 1895, Police Captain Max F. Schmittberger testified before a state commission that New York City's entire police department was "rotten to the core." It took $600 to make an officer a sergeant, $14,000 to make him a captain. "It's either politics or money," he stated, "that moves a man to higher command." Describing the collapse of the justice system in the nation's largest city, he used this phrase: "The pillars of the church are falling and have fallen."

Three years after Captain Schmittberger's testimony, another citizen, fulfilling a boyhood dream, joined the New York Police Department. This is his story.

When I got to be twenty-one years of age I tried to get on the police force, and a politician told me that he would put me on for $300. I had been working as a clerk for a junkman in Pearl Street and had saved a little money and I agreed to pay $300. I gave it to the politician in the back room of a saloon on William Street, and he counted the money and said that he would see me through. He told the proprietor of the place to enclose the money in an envelope, and put it in his safe, which was done.

I made my application and waited three months, but was turned down.

The politician told me that I would have to raise $300 more, and so I went back to clerking till the beginning of

1898 when I was ready for another attempt to get on the force. I made application to the Civil Service Commissioners and received a copy of the requirements, which seemed to show that I was not eligible.

Two policemen told me that the civil service people were square, and that money had nothing to do with passing examinations. I found that there was a fight on under the surface between the civil service schools and the politicians because the schools were putting men on the force who had paid nothing to their leaders.

I told my district leader that I was going to the school and he swore at me.

Six months after I had entered the school I was examined by the Civil Service Commissioners and passed with *81* percent physical and *83* percent mental, and a month later I was appointed by the police commissioner. That was in November, *1898.*

I was assigned to duty in the precinct where I lived, and reported to the captain, who put me on probation for *30* days. Each week day I attended the police school of instruction, where I kept up athletics and learned drill and rules, and each night I went out with a policeman, who "broke me in" to the duties, and whom I assisted in making arrests.

The politician met me on the street, shook his fist in my face, and swore that he would have me dismissed from the force if I didn't "put up." I told him he was a "has been," and that one had to "put up" now. He made trouble for me two or three times after that by means of a sergeant who worked one night and day and a roundsman who was always reporting me. Finally I got myself transferred out of his district, when I thought I was safe, but he kept after me by means of another leader, till at last I gave him $200 to "call it square."

The influence of the politicians over the police force has been growing weaker all the time, and some of the sergeants and captains now refuse to take orders from the district leaders.

The politicians' "pull" is founded on the fact that they make the mayor who makes the police commissioner. So when they elect a mayor they ask for a commissioner who will suit them, and when he is in office they can make it very hot for a captain who tries to enforce blue laws. They can move the captains around, putting one who does as he is told in a place where he can make $30,000 a year in addition to salary, and another in a place where he cannot make a cent extra.

So if a policeman disturbs "good people who are paying tribute" the district leader complains to the captain of the precinct, and if he does not mend matters a complaint of the captain is made to the commissioner. But this seldom happens. The patrolman who insisted on enforcing all the laws would be an idiot. He would not last a month, and would be thrown out a broken and disgraced man. His officers and comrades would see to that.

How far this business of protecting people who violate laws goes I don't know. It used to include pickpockets, tin-horn gamblers with brace games, bunco men, green goods and knock-out-drops operators, and burglars—pretty nearly all sorts of regular operators. It isn't anything like as complete now as it used to be. Still there are pickpockets now operating about the Bridge, and how could they do it unless the police were fixed?

Some are let work and some are taken in, and there must

be a reason for the difference of treatment. Pickpockets, like detectives, work in couples, and I've known one to come up to a pair of plainclothes men, and say:

"The other fellow has $150."

One of the detectives collars the other pickpocket, and says: "I guess I'll have to take you up to the station house and 'mug' you (take photograph for Rogue's Gallery)."

"Can't we fix it up?" says the pickpocket. "I have $75."

"All right," says the detective, and takes the $75 and the pickpocket trots on. Soon hears footsteps behind him, and another detective catches him. "Hey! What are you doing here? I'll have to take you in," says the second detective, and the pickpocket is collared again, and has to give up the other $75 to get off. He goes away kicking himself.

Now, what did the first pickpocket get for betraying his partner? He must get something, for thieves have to live, and it costs money to support their families. The city isn't paying their salaries. It seems to stand to reason that the detectives must pay them by allowing them to work, and I suppose [it is the same] with the other criminals as with the pickpockets. But I don't pretend to know, and I'm sure that no one man knows all ends of this business of "protection," there's so much secrecy even between those most deeply engaged in it.

Since the last election we have had in office commissioners who could not be used by politicians to punish a man for doing his duty, and that's all right so far as it goes. But the men and their officers know perfectly well that the politicians are only down for the moment, and that they are coming back to power, so why should policemen make trouble for themselves by opposition to the present system.

That's the way we patrolmen look at the matter, so we go with the tide, taking what comes and not seeing any more than is good for us to see.

As I went around with the experienced policeman during my probation he taught me all the ropes, and explained that the greatest danger for a young man was from the temptation to arrest people who were "putting up."

"If you do that," he said, "the sergeant will work you forty-eight hours at a stretch, and finally break you."

It didn't take me long to find out that the sergeant could keep me on the go till I dropped if it suited him. That was when I went on regular duty at the end of a month. I arrested a saloonkeeper who forgot me, but who had put up for the wardman and the inspector's man. I got a hint to leave the man alone after that, but I wanted to make him understand that I Had something to say as well as the big fellows. I took him in again for violating the Sunday law. He was discharged. Soon after that I came off duty and went on reserve. I went upstairs to the dormitory to sleep, having been on patrol for sixteen hours. I had not been in bed ten minutes when the sergeant called me down to the desk, and sent me out to see about some boys annoying householders ten blocks away. It was a fake report. When I came back he sent me out to a fire, and after that he found another special call to keep me busy till I had to go on patrol again. There are plenty of these special calls at a busy station house, and the sergeant can always make some if he wants them. I squared matters by apologizing to the saloonkeeper.

Before I got on the force I had heard that policemen made a deal of money in addition to their salaries, and after I got fairly to work I found that I was in it.

Of course, when promotions are paid for, the money had to come from "put ups." In Manhattan as much as $10,000 has sometimes been paid for a captaincy, but that is nothing if a man gets the right kind of a precinct where he can make from $20,000 to $50,000 a year. As I get them the rates for protection in Manhattan have been as follows per month:

Pool rooms, from $300 to $500; salons, from $10 to $40; gambling houses, from $100 to $2,000; disorderly houses, $20 to $100; push carts, $2 per week each.

There's plenty of other "graft" that I don't know about; for instance, the detectives down in Wall Street make a lot of money somehow.

The push cart peddlers' money is collected by one of themselves. He goes among the carts and marks the stand of the man who has paid with white chalk, and the stand of the man who has not paid with blue chalk. The ignorant peddler does not notice.

Along comes the policeman on post and looks at the carts. When he sees a blue mark on a cart he with his club poles the back off the peddler that owns it, moving him on while he lets his comrades stand.

In some of the precincts where there is plenty of "graft," the man who is violating the law pays the patrolman for closing his eyes, the captain for not breaking the patrolman, and the inspector for not breaking the captain. These are separate amounts. Say the patrolman get $5 a month, the captain and inspector would get $20 each.

The most I ever made on any post was $156 a month. That was downtown in Manhattan on a beat that was about a mile and a half long. Every saloonkeeper on my post used to put up $5 a month for me and my partner in addition to the money given to the captain's agent—the inspector had no one collecting. There were twenty-five of these saloons and five gambling places, three of which gave me $10 a month, while two paid $5. From the women I and my partner, who patrolled the beat when I was off, got a total of about $75 a month. Of course, there were many who tried to do business without paying, but they soon found themselves in a hole because we enforced the law against them. Some patrolmen have made as high as $250 a month.

Besides the presents of money which naturally make policemen feel kindly disposed toward the givers there is free liquor. It is everywhere offered to the policemen, and it trips a good many of them up.

After a man has been on the force a little while he knows all the people who are "putting up," and grows to be very friendly with them. There are twenty places on my beat where I can tap at a side door and get a drink, and there are nearly as many where I can go in a back room and sleep while some one watches to give me warning if the roundsman comes in sight. So the temptation to take it easy and have a good time is very great, and on bad nights the policeman need not patrol his post unless he wants to.

New York policemen are just as honest as any other set of men, and this system of bribery is not their fault. It is the fault of the fool laws made for the benefit of old women who don't understand human nature. The laws pretend to try to abolish gambling and disorderly houses and to close drinking places on the only weekly holiday. That is all hypocrisy. Men always will gamble and drink. In the great cities of Europe there is a license system. If that were in force here it would put a stop to police bribery.

Life as a Coal Miner

In 1902 the United Mine Workers in the anthracite region of Pennsylvania called a strike for higher pay and union recognition and 15,000 miners walked out of the coal pits. Mine owners responded by calling in strikebreakers and soon there were shootings, bombings, and riots. As the cold weather approached, the UMW proposed arbitration.

The coal operators rejected it. President George F. Baer of the Reading Railroad voiced their views when he declared: "The rights and interests of the laboring man will be protected and cared for—not by labor agitators, but by the Christian men to whom God in His infinite wisdom has given the control of the property interests of the country."

Life As a Coal Miner

George F. Baer's words reveal the attitudes of one side. But the words of the anonymous coal miner who participated in this strike form a fascinating contrast and deserve a place in the historical record.

I am thirty-five years old, married, the father of four children, and have lived in the coal region all my life. Twenty-three of these years have been spent working in and around the mines. My father was a miner. He died ten years ago from "miners' asthma."

Three of my brothers are miners; none of us had any opportunities to acquire an education. We were sent to school (such a school as there was in those days) until we were about twelve years of age, and then we were put into the screen room of a breaker to pick slate. From there we went inside the mines as driver boys. As we grew, we were taken on as laborers, where we served until able to call ourselves miners. We were given work in the breasts and gangways. There were five of us boys. One lies in the cemetery—fifty tons of top rock dropped on him. He was killed three weeks after he got his job as a miner—a month before he was to be married.

In the fifteen years I have worked as a miner I have earned the average rate of wages any of us coal heavers get. Today I am little better off than when I started to do for myself. I have $100 on hand; I am not in debt; I hope to be able to weather the strike without going hungry.

I am only one of the hundreds you see on the street every day. The muscles on my arms are no harder, the callous on my palms no deeper than my neighbor's whose entire life has been spent in the coal region. By years I am only thirty-five. But look at the marks on my body; look at the lines of worriment on my forehead; see the gray hairs on my head and in my mustache; take my general appearance, and you'll think I'm ten years older.

You need not wonder why. Day in and day out, from Monday morning to Saturday evening, between the rising and the setting of the sun, I am in the underground workings of the coal mines. From the seams water trickles into the ditches along the gangways; if not water, it is the gas which hurls us to eternity and the props and timbers to a chaos.

Our daily life is not a pleasant one. When we put on our oil soaked suit in the morning we can't guess all the dangers which threaten our lives. We walk sometimes miles to the place—to the man way or traveling way, or to the mouth of the shaft on top of the slope. And then we enter the darkened chambers of the mines. On our right and on our left we see the logs that keep up the top and support the sides which may crush us into shapeless masses, as they have done to many of our comrades.

We get old quickly. Powder, smoke, after-damp, bad air—all combine to bring furrows to our faces and asthma to our lungs.

I did not strike because I wanted to; I struck because I had to. A miner—the same as any other workman—must earn fair living wages, or he can't live. And it is not how much you get that counts. It is how much what you get will buy. I have gone through it all, and I think my case is a good sample.

Life As a Coal Miner

I was married in *1890*, when I was twenty-three years old—quite a bit above the age when we miner boys get into double harness. The woman I married is like myself. She was born beneath the shadow of dirt bank; her chances for school weren't any better than mine; but she did have to learn how to keep house on a certain amount of money. After we paid the preacher for tying the knot we had just $185 in cash, good health, and the good wishes of many friends to start us off.

Our cash was exhausted in buying furniture for housekeeping. In *1890* work was not so plentiful, and by the time our first baby came there was room for much doubt as to how we would pull out. Low wages, and not much over half time in those years, made us hustle. In *1890-91*, from June to May *1*, I earned $368.72. That represented eleven months' work, or an average of $33.52 per month. Our rent was $10 per month; store not less than $20. And then I had my oil suits and gum boots to pay for. The result was that after the first year and a half of our married life we were in debt. Not much, of course, and not as much as many of my neighbors, men of larger families, and some who made less money, or in whose case there had been sickness or accident or death. These are all things which a miner must provide for.

In *1896* my wife was sick eleven weeks. The doctor came to my house almost every day. He charged me $20 for his services. There was medicine to buy. I paid the drugstore $18 in that time. Her mother nursed her, and we kept a girl in the kitchen at $1.50 a week, which cost me $15 for ten weeks, besides the additional living expenses.

In *1897*, just a year afterward, I had a severer trial. And mind, in those years, we were only working about half time.

But in the fall of that year one of my brothers struck a gas feeder. There was a terrible explosion. He was hurled downward in the breast and covered with the rush of coal and rock. I was working only three breasts away from him and for a moment was unable to realize what had occurred. Myself and a hundred others were soon at work, however, and in a short while we found him, horrible burned over his whole body, his laborer dead alongside of him.

He was my brother. He was single and had been boarding. He had no home of his own. I didn't want him taken to the hospital, so I directed the driver of the ambulance to take him to my house. Besides being burned, his right arm and left leg were broken, and he was hurt internally. The doctors—there were two at the house when we got there—said he would die. But he didn't. He is living and a miner today. But he lay in bed just fourteen weeks, and was unable to work for seven weeks after he got out of bed. He had no money when he was hurt except the amount represented by his pay. All of the expenses for doctors, medicine, extra help, and his living were borne by me, except $25, which another brother gave me. The last one had none to give. Poor work, low wages, and a sickly woman for a wife had kept him scratching for his own family.

It is nonsense to say I was not compelled to keep him, that I could have sent him to a hospital or the almshouse. We are American citizens and we don't go to hospitals and poorhouses.

Let us look at things as they are today, or as they were before the strike commenced.

My last pay envelope shows my wages, after my laborer, powder, oil, and other expenses were taken off, were $29.47; that was my earning for two weeks, and that was extra good. The laborer for the same time got some $21. His wages are a trifle over $10 a week for six full days. Before the strike of 1900 he was paid in this region $1.70 per day, or $10.20 a week. If the ten percent raise had been given, as we expected, his wages would be $1.87 per day, or $11.22 per week, or an increase of $1.02 per week. But we all know that under the present system he doesn't get any eleven dollars.

Well, as I said my wages were $29.47 for the two weeks, or at the rate of $58.94 per month. My rent is $10.50 per month. My coal costs me almost $4 per month. We burn a little over a ton a month on an average and it costs us over $3 per ton. Light does not cost so much; we use coal oil altogether.

When it comes down to groceries is where you get hit the hardest. Everybody knows the cost of living has been extremely high all winter. Butter has been 32, 36, and 38cents a pound; eggs as high as 32 cents a dozen; ham, 12 and 16 cents a pound; potatoes away up to a dollar, and cabbage not less than a cent a pound. Fresh meat need not be counted. Flour and sugar did not advance, but they were about the only staples that didn't. Anyhow, my store bill for those two weeks was $11. That makes $22 per month. The butcher gets $6 per month. Add them all, and it costs me, just to live, $42.50. That leaves me $17 per month to keep my family in clothes, to pay my church dues and to keep the industrial insurance going. My insurance alone costs me 55 cents a week, or $2.20 a month.

The coal president never allows his stable boss to cut the amount of fodder allotted to his mules. He insists on so many quarts of oats and corn to the meal and so much hay in the evening. The mule must be fed; the miner may be, if he works hard enough and earns money to buy the grub.

Company stores are of the time that has been. Their existence ended two years ago. But we've got a system growing up that threatens to be just as bad. Let me explain. Over a year ago I was given a breast to drive at one of our mines and was glad to get it. My wife took her cash and went around the different places to buy. When I went to the office for my first pay the "super" met me and asked me if I didn't know his wife's brother George kept a store. I answered, "Yes," and wanted to know what that had to do with it.

"Nothing, only I thought I'd call your attention to it," he answered.

No more was said then. But the next day I got a quiet tip that my breast was to be abandoned. This set me thinking. I went to the boss and, after a few words, told him my wife had found brother-in-law George's store and that she liked it much better than where she had bought before. I told him the other store didn't sell the right kind of silk waists, and their patent-leather shoes were away back. Brother-in-law George had the right kind of stuff and, of course, we were willing to pay a few cents more to get just what we wanted.

That was sarcastic, but it's the cash that had the influence. I have had work at that colliery ever since. I know my living costs me from *10* to *15* percent extra. But I kept my job, which meant a good deal.

Now you must take into consideration that I am a contract miner and that my earnings are more than the wages of three-fourths of the other fellows at the same colliery. It is not that I am a favorite with the boss. I just struck a good breast. Maybe next month my wages would be from two to six seven dollars less.

In the days of Pardee, Coxe, Fagley, Fulton, Dewees, Paterson, Riley, Repplier, Graeber, and a hundred others, men were better paid than they have ever been since the centralization ideas of the late Franklin B. Gowen became fixed institutions in the anthracite counties. It may be true that in the days of the individual operation the cost per ton of mining coal was less that it is today. But it is not right that the entire increase in the cost of mining be charged to the miner. That is what is being done, if you count the reductions made in wages.

We miners do not participate in the high prices of coal. The operators try to prove otherwise by juggling with figures, but their proving has struck a fault, and the drill shows no coal in that section. One-half of the price paid for a ton of coal in New York or Philadelphia goes into the profit pocket of the mine owner, either as a carrier or miner.

We all know that the price of coal has advanced in the past twenty years. We also know that wages are less, that the cost of living is higher. I remember the time, when I was a wee lad, my father used to get his coal for $1 per ton. Now I pay $3. In those days we lads used to go to the dirt banks and pick a load of coal, and it cost our parents only a half a dollar to get it hauled home. We dare not do that now. Then we did not need gum boots, safety lamps or any such things as that; and for all of them we must now pay out of wages that have been reduced.

Our condition can be no worse; it might and must be better. The luxuries of the rich we do not ask; we do want butter for our bread and meat for our soup. We do not want silk and laces for our wives and daughters. But we want to earn enough to buy them a clean calico once in a while. Our boys are not expecting automobiles and membership cards in clubs of every city, but they want their fathers to earn enough to keep them at school until they have a reasonably fair education.

Nat Love: From Southern Slave to Western Cowpuncher

Nat Love, known as Deadwood Dick, was born in a Tennessee slave cabin before the Civil War. He was one of 40,000 Black, white, Indian, and Latino cowpunchers who drove cattle up the Chisholm Trail. With obvious relish and swaggering self-assurance, Love fought outlaws, Indians, and lawmen; braved hailstones, swollen rivers, and rampaging cattle herds; battled wild animals; and lived to tell his tale in typical western braggadocio.

Actually, most cowpunchers of the nineteenth century had a terribly dull, sometimes hazardous, and always low-paying job. Excessive boasting and gunplay became the means of reconciling a hearty, swashbuckling personality with te-dious work and long, lonely nights on the western prairies.

The tall tales related by men like Nat Love helped create the enduring myth of the cowboy, the great American hero.

In an old log cabin, on my Master's plantation in Davidson County in Tennessee in June, *1854*, I first saw the light of day. The exact date of my birth I never knew, because in those days no count was kept of such trivial matters as the birth of a slave baby. . . .

It was on the tenth day of February, *1869*, that I left the old home near Nashville, Tennessee. I was at that time about fifteen years old, and though while young in years the hard work and farm life had made me strong and hearty, much beyond my years, and I had full confidence in my-self as being able to take care of myself and make my way.

I at once struck out for Kansas of which I had heard something. And believing it was a good place in which to seek employment. It was in the West, and it was the great West I wanted to see, and so by walking and occasional lifts from farmers going my way and taking advantage of ev-erything that promised to assist me on my way, I eventu-ally brought up at Dodge City, Kansas, which at that time was a typical frontier city, with great many saloons, dance halls, and gambling houses, and very little of anything else.

When I arrived the town was full of cowboys from the surrounding ranches, and from Texas and other parts of the West. As Kansas was a great cattle center and market, the wild cowboy, prancing horses of which I was very fond, and the wild life generally, all had their attractions for me, and I decided to try for a place with them....

During the big round-ups it was our duty to pick out our brand, and then send them home under the charge of our cowboys, likewise the newly branded stock. After each brand was cut out and started homeward, we had to stay with the round-up to see that strays from the different herds from the surrounding country did not again get mixed up, until the different home ranges were reached. This work employed a large number of cowboys, who lived, ate, and often slept in the saddle, as they covered many hundreds of miles in a very short space of time. This was made possible as every large cattleman had relays of horses sent out over the country where we might be expected to touch, and so we could always count on finding a fresh horse awaiting us at the end of a twenty-five or a fifty-mile ride. But for us brand readers there was no rest; we merely changed our saddles and outfit to a fresh horse and were again on the go. After the general round-up was over, cowboy sports and a good time generally was in order for those engaged in it.

In order to get the cattle together in the first general round-up, we would have to ride for hundreds of miles over the country in search of the long-horn steers and old cows that had drifted from the home range during the winter and were now scattered to the four winds of heaven. As soon as they were found they were started off under the care of cowboys for the place agreed upon for the general round-up, whether they belonged to us or not, while the test of us continues the search. All the cowboys from the many different outfits working this way enabled us to soon get all the strays rounded up in one great herd in which the cattle of a dozen different owners were mixed up together. It then became our duty to cut out our different herds and start them homewards. Then we had to brand the young stock that had escaped that ordeal at the hands of the range riders. On finding the strays and starting them homewards, we had to keep up the search, because notwithstanding the fact that we had done range riding or line riding all winter, a large number of cattle would manage to evade the vigilance of the cowboys and get away. These must all be accounted for at the great round-up, as they stood for dollars and cents, profit and loss to the great cattle kings of the West.

In going after these strayed and perhaps stolen cattle we boys always provided ourselves with everything we needed, including plenty of grub, as sometimes we would be gone for nearly two months and sometimes much longer. It was not an uncommon occurrence for us to have shooting trouble over our different brands. In such disputes the boys would kill each other if others did not interfere in time to prevent it, because in those days on the great cattle ranges there was no law but the law of might, and all disputes were settled with a forty-five Colt pistol. In such cases the man who was quickest on the draw and whose eye was the best, pretty generally got the decision. Therefore it was of the greatest importance that the cowboy should understand his gun, its capabilities, and its shooting qualities. A cowboy would never carry anything but the very best gun obtainable, as his life depended on it often. After securing a good gun the cowboy had to learn how to use it, if he did not already know how. In doing so no trouble or expense was spared, and I know there were very few poor shots on the ranges over which we rode and they used the accomplishment to protect themselves and their employer's cattle from the Indian thieves and the white desperadoes who infested the cattle country, and who lost no opportunity to stampede the herds and run off large numbers of them. Whenever this happened it generally resulted in a long chase and a fierce fight in which someone was sure to get hurt, and hurt badly. But that fact did not bother us in the least. It was all simply our duty and our business for which we were paid and paid good, and so we accepted things as they came, always ready for it whatever it might be, and always taking pride in our work in which we always tried to excel.

We arrived in Deadwood in good condition without having had any trouble with the Indians on the way up. We turned our cattle over to their new owners at once, then proceeded to take in the town. The next morning, July 4th, the gamblers and mining men made up a purse of $200 for a roping contest between the cowboys that were then in town, and as it was holiday nearly all the cowboys for miles around were assembled there that day. It did not take long to arrange the details for the contest and contestants, six of them being colored cowboys, including myself. Our trail boss was chosen to pick out the mustangs from a herd of wild horses just off the range, and he picked out twelve of the most wild and vicious horses that he could find.

The conditions of the contest were that each of us who were mounted was to rope, throw, tie, bridle and saddle, and mount the particular horse picked for us in the shortest time possible. The man accomplishing the feat in the quickest time was to be declared the winner.

It seems to me that the horse chosen for me was the most vicious of the lot. Everything being in readiness, the "45" cracked and we all sprang forward together, each of us making for our particular mustang.

I roped, threw, tied, bridled, saddled, and mounted my mustang in exactly nine minutes from the crack of the gun. The time of the next nearest competitor was twelve minutes and thirty seconds. This gave me the record and championship of the West, which I held up to the time I quit the business in *1890*, and my record has never been beaten. It is worthy of passing remark that I never had a horse pitch with me so much as that mustang, but I never stopped sticking my spurs in him and using my quirt on his flanks until I proved his master. Right there the assembled crowd named me Deadwood Dick and proclaimed me champion roper of the western cattle country.

The roping contest over, a dispute arose over the shooting question with the result that a contest was arranged for the afternoon, as there happened to be some of the best shots with rifle and revolver in the West present that day. Among them were Stormy Jim, who claimed the championship; Powder Horn Bill, who had the reputation of never missing what he shot at; also White Head, a half-breed, who generally hit what he shot at, and many other men who knew how to handle a rifle or *45* Colt.

The range was measured off *100* and *250* yards for the rifle and *150* for the Colt *45*. At this distance a bull's-eye about the size of an apple was put up. Each man was to have *14* shots at each range with the rifle and *12* shots with the Colt *45*. I placed every one of my *14* shots with the rifle in the bull's-eye with ease, all shots being made from the hip; but with the *45* Colt I missed it twice, only placing *10* shots in the small circle, Stormy Jim being my nearest competitor, only placing *8* bullets in the bull's-eye clear, and the rest being quite close, while with the *45* he placed *5* bullets in the charmed circle. This gave me the champion-ship of rifle and revolver shooting as well as the roping contest, and for that day I was the hero of Deadwood, and the purse of $*200* which I had won on the roping contest went toward keeping things moving, and they did move as only a large crowd of cattle men can move things. This lasted for several days when most of the cattle men had to return to their respective ranches, as it was the busy sea-son; accordingly our outfit began to make preparations to return to Arizona.

Bibliographical Notes

The selections in this volume are from a number of sources. The African American cowpuncher's story appears in Nat Love, *The Life and Adventures of Nat Love, Better Known in the Cattle Country as "Deadwood Dick," By Himself*, published by himself (1907). Elias Garza's account is from an interview in 1926 conducted by the Social Research Council, and appears in Manuel Gamio, ed., *The Mexican Immigrant: His Life Story* (University of Chicago Press, 1931). Anna Louise Strong's recollection is from her autobiography, *I Change Worlds* (Henry Holt, 1931). Bernardo Vega's selection appears in his *Memoirs of Bernardo Vega*, edited by Cesar Andreu Iglesias, translated by Juan Flores

(Monthly Review Press reprint, 1984). Elizabeth Gurley Flynn's excerpt is from her autobiography, *The Rebel Girl, My First Life* 1906–1926 (International Publishers, 1955).

I am particularly indebted to Professor Jose Luis Marin, Chair of the Department of Puerto Rican/Latin American Studies Studies at John Jay College, who provided a prepublication copy of his fascinating paper "Indiginous Hawaiians Under Statehood: Lessons for Puerto Rico," *Centro Journal: Journal of the Center for Puerto Rican Studies* (Vol. 11, #2, Spring, 2000) and for helping to clarify connections between domestic events and U.S. foreign policy from Puerto Rico to Hawaii.

Many first person accounts were located decades ago in a copy of Hamilton Holt, ed., *The Life Stories of Undistinguished Americans, As Told by Themselves* (1906) in a secondhand bookstore on Fourth Avenue in New York. A reformer and founding member of the NAACP, Holt's compendium reprinted sixteen of what he called "Lifelets" that had appeared in *The Independent*, a magazine that he edited. The files of *The Independent* yielded six dozen other "Lifelets," often personal perspectives that seldom appear in schools.

At the beginning of the twentieth century, Holt had shifted the editorial focus of *The Independent* to ordinary people, who, he was convinced, were coming into their own. For literary, historical, and sociological reasons, he wanted to preserve their own record of passage. Edwin E. Slosson, literary editor of *The Independent*, vouched for the "Lifelets" accuracy and saw them as necessary for "the spirit of democracy, the discovery of the importance of the average man." He concluded: "It is the undistinguished people who move the world, or who prevent it from moving."

Bibliographical Notes

In addition to those listed above, the following excellent books and articles have been very helpful:

Oscar Ameringer, *If You Don't Weaken: The Autobiography of Oscar Ameringer* (University of Oklahoma Press, 1973).

Otto L. Bettmann, *The Good Old Days—They Were Terrible!* (Random House, 1974).

Carlos Buloson, *America Is in the Heart* (University of Washington Press, 1988).

Franklin Folsom, *Impatient Armies of the Poor* (University Press of Colorado, 1991).

Ray Ginger, *The Age of Excess: The United States from 1877 to 1914* (Macmillan, 1965).

William D. Haywood, *The Autobiography of Big Bill Haywood* (International Publishers, 1927).

Matthew Josephson, *The Robber Barons* (Harcourt Brace and World, 1934).

Mark Sullivan, *Our Times: The United States 1900–1925*, 4 vols. (Charles Scribner's Sons, 1926).

Harvey Swados, ed., *Years of Conscience, The Muckrakers* (World Publishing, 1962).

Editors, *U.S. News*, "Our Century: Having Their Say: In a Remarkable Oral History, America's 100-Year-Olds Tell The Story of a Nation's Journey to Modern Times," Special Double Issue, September 30, 1995.

Howard Zinn, *A People's History of the United States* (Harper and Row, 1984).

Nat Love, cowhand

Rose Schneiderman speaks at a street rally

Women strikers in Chicago, 1911

Laborers of many tongues united in their union

Children marched in New Jersey in support of striking mothers and fathers in the Industrial Workers of the World (IWW)

Italian immigrants arrive in New York

Japanese immigrants on the way to jobs in Hawaii in 1904

A Macon, Georgia, textile mill, 1909

A Yazoo, Mississippi, mill foreman and young workers

Child laborers in a factory

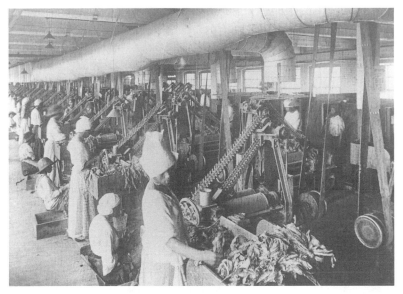

A tobacco factory employing African-American women

Irish-American coal mining boys in Pennsylvania, 1911

A Massachusetts textile factory in 1912 (Lewis Hine photo)

Southern convict labor camp for African Americans in 1910

A public school class for immigrant children in the 1890s

Life on a tenement fire escape

A school for Native Americans in the State of Washington

Hester Street, New York City slums